Twitcn

Streaming

Basic Brand Growth and Setup Tricks

(How to Make Money Online Right Now From Home Using Twitch)

Pedro Brown

Published By **John Kembrey**

Pedro Brown

All Rights Reserved

Twitch Streaming: Basic Brand Growth and Setup Tricks (How to Make Money Online Right Now From Home Using Twitch)

ISBN   978-1-998038-31-2

No part of this guidebook shall be reproduced in any form without permission in writing from the publisher except in the case of brief quotations embodied in critical articles or reviews.

Legal & Disclaimer

The information contained in this book is not designed to replace or take the place of any form of medicine or professional medical advice. The information in this book has been provided for educational & entertainment purposes only.

The information contained in this book has been compiled from sources deemed reliable, and it is accurate to the best of the Author's knowledge; however, the Author cannot guarantee its accuracy and validity and cannot be held liable for any errors or omissions. Changes are periodically made to this book. You must consult your doctor or get professional medical advice before using any of the suggested remedies, techniques, or information in this book.

Table Of Contents

Chapter 1: How To Make Money As A Twitch Novice?

Twitch is, by using way of using an prolonged shot, the maximum mainstream streaming level in the international for game enthusiasts. The observers and decorations profits thru Twitch's essential framework and its massive userbase. While Twitch is most usually related to computer recreation streaming, there are a whole lot of brilliant varieties of transfer available at the administration now. Just as videogame net-based totally genuinely, floods of every stay seller playing clubs and the definitely automated online club are handy. Some podcasters have even taken to the degree to spread their substance sooner or later of the Covid-19 lockdown.

Just due to the fact the level's a remarkable framework and large patron base, it has moreover showed well-known with decorations since it offers them with numerous opportunities to monetize their substance, so if you're considering a manner to herald cash via your Twitch movement, that's what you need to understand.

Tips And Donations

For streamers who aren't participants and are, on this way, incapable of creating the most of Twitch's Bits software, there are however a few strategies that you can request gives out of your visitors. The most truthful method of doing this is through an outsider level like Stripe or PayPal. Both of these stages make it easy to ship cash straightforwardly to you. You can likewise impart a hook up with your supporters a great way to take them at once to the net web page they will use to deliver you cash.

Numerous streamers have positioned that defining a gift purpose and giving a practical demonstrating how near the goal they're is a a success technique of urging extra traffic to offer. You can likewise use Twitch cautions to aid more presents from site visitors.

Patreon is a famous degree for creatives who want to open up another profits circulate. In addition to the reality that Patreon makes it smooth for your site visitors to offer in your channel, however it likewise empowers you to provide them degree selective substance as an impetus.

Subscribers

This is each other opportunity just open to the people who are important for Twitch's Affiliate or Partnership applications. When you have tried out the form of responsibilities, a 'buy-in' seize will consequently be delivered in your internet web page, and your viewers can be part of your channel. Supporters benefit admittance to top class-virtually highlights for that decorations channel, for example, custom acts out and specific blessings—in the intervening time, the decoration gets the possibility to divide the rate of membership down the center with Twitch. Memberships run in fee from $4.Ninety 9 as much as $24.Ninety nine each month, so that it will body a noteworthy wellspring of repeating pay for the most mainstream Twitch streamers.

Bits

Bits are surprisingly much like Twitch's own 'in-exercise' coins. This isn't always virtual coins, however it is virtual coins. Each Twitch Bit is sincerely worth 1 penny ($zero.01), and that they may take delivery of to decorations through the extent's cheering expert. Viewers can rent cheers to provide singular Bits or a extraordinary many Bits on the double. A few site visitors will employ them to compensate, specifically skillful interactivity. Others need to make use of them in moderate of the decoration themselves. Viewers have the opportunity of connecting a message to their cheer and might appoint 'Cheermotes' – energized acts out.

If that you are feeling that every cheer you get will add $0.01 on your file balance, that you could then be able to get better for coins via PayPal on the same time as your parity arrives at a specific limit, all spherical completed, you are a affordable character. Sadly, Twitch isn't cheap; it is scarcely even an individual. Just taking an exciting streamer receives a reduce of the benefits from spent cheers. Notwithstanding, for streamers with an massive after, Bits are a huge wellspring of profits.

Merchandise

If you have got were given a big internet following in 2020, your line of products is almost required now. Creating your product is simple these days. The maximum vital element you need to create is the automatic plans. You could possibly then be capable of provide your gadgets to set up to make use of a custom product keep like Spreadshop. The first rate difficulty about print-to-set up stock is which you do no longer need to pay for creation forthright.

This implies you do not need to strain over carrying out with a carport brimming with an unsold product which you haven't any utilization for. You moreover do not need to strain this sort of first rate amount over your capability to offer for your crowd. Huge numbers of the best Twitch streamers these days are marking now. Consolidating your Gamertag or on-line deal with with an less expensive sensible to create a brand will moreover help you with selling your products.

Sponsorship

Twitch is currently the finest streaming degree in the world and is with the useful resource of a big margin the most well-known choice for each expert and amateur streamers. There had been endeavors at starting contending degrees, but Twitch is this kind of triumphing energy that any contenders have a hard, however no longer not feasible challenge in advance. Indeed, even the ones optionally available administrations which have found out the manner to attract a part of Twitch's greater names to their foundation have been no longer able to the us the goliath from its seat.

There are countless sponsorship open doors for high-quality decorations on

Twitch. On the off hazard that your waft is mainstream sufficient, at that component, the ones open doors will begin to come to you. Nonetheless, if you are installation to find out leads all by myself and method possible backers on your stress, you may think that its masses much less hard to companion with sensible customers.

Game Sales

Streamers who're crucial for Twitch's accomplice responsibilities can sell video games and in-sport matters the use of their pages. Partaking streamers will get a five% slice of any deals made via their internet net page. This cycle is altogether mechanized. If you're selling the profile, you'll certainly get your reduce of the benefits. When you are gaming, and that allows selling in-recreation topics thru Twitch, a crate will be blanketed under your circulate. Your traffic might possibly then be able to make buys with out leaving your flow.

There are numerous motives that Twitch has hooked up to be this sort of hit among streamers and their crowds, yet a first-rate hassle of Twitch's appeal is that it empowers streamers and substance makers to herald cash. The income streams I sincerely have diagnosed above are quality a willpower of the severa open doors available on Twitch.

Gaming is what inside the starting launched Twitch. It became the primary draw of the platform for a long time. Even these days, people need to music in often to study gaming. The well-known instructions, in phrases of likability, are enterprise categories: Fortnite and League of Legends.

It's vital to look; however, that 1/three at the agenda, with above 650 million hours appeared and a YoY increase rate of 40 percentage, changed into the Just Chatting problem — one that does not want to do a little element with gamer subculture and video games. A few vast topics, most conspicuously, that you don't need to stall out growing terrible gaming content material fabric if there's a few issue you're substantially progressed at. Here are guidelines that permit you to with getting subsided right into a extraordinary substance class — or a couple.

Make experience of whether or no longer or not you need to be an collection of decorations or maintain on with one class

A few people will leap amongst gaming, talks, and spilling in a hurry as a element of an collection of substance method. Others will 0 in on talking on my own, or making workmanship, or playing a solitary undertaking, or gambling a type of video video games. As an assortment of decorations, your individual is a vast draw. In case you are, to a extra amount, an engaged decoration, your perception, and skills will assist you in constructing a set of humans.

Stream what you need

The odds are that you may invest some electricity gushing to a chunk crowd. Beginnings may be immoderate, and streaming can, in some instances, appear like a frightening mission to succeed upon every viewer in flip. The ideal approach to stay with it's miles through streaming some thing you like doing, no matter whether or not or not it's an hobby of yours or a recreation you want playing.

Cautiously pick out the video games you need to transport

The most famous video video video games have bunches of traffic but additionally masses of putting in vicinity channels rushing to them. New deliveries can swell rapidly, as obvious inside the 2019 example of overcoming adversity of Apex Legends. A exquisite stunt is to utilize gadgets, for instance, Quizzical Pixel's What to Stream, to discover video video video games which have first rate viewership; but, not many channels streaming them.

Consider a skip-pastime forte; individuals will find out charming

You don't want to paste to at least one class to expose into a completely an entire lot seemed decoration with a incredible after. You may be a speedrunner who desires to traverse video games as fast as need to reasonably be predicted. You can be a profoundly critical gamer who specialists recreation really to duel people. You might also additionally moreover flourish as a network grasp who makes experience of pastime mechanics and allows different human beings end up top notch at games.

The pick out substance you can produce usually

Since consistency is vital almost about streaming, the proper method to do it is to try to adhere to a timetable, however a wonderful deal as should pretty be expected. If the substance you need to make does not allow you to motion robotically, it's miles extremely good to abstain from streaming that form of substance. That is in case you do now not plan to consist of some unique kind of substance to your portfolio which can fill in the holes.

Chapter 2: What Is Twitch?

Individuals love looking recordings. They appreciate looking and making live recordings significantly greater in slight of their issue of suddenness. That is likely why Twitch is so well-known. Twitch is the precept live streaming degree. Think YouTube, however, with simply live recordings. If you have were given in no way recognized about it, do not stress. That is everyday. Twitch has a strong factor crowd of net-primarily based game enthusiasts. The reality is the maximum of Twitch customers are gamers who host and provide eSports events and issues on the degree. The fact is that it's miles the area's biggest net activity net-based totally level.

However, that doesn't endorse that Twitch has nothing to carry to the desk to different substance makers. You'll find out a big range of recordings on Twitch, remembering demos and educational wearing sports for DIY, cooking, cosmetics, modern-day expressions, and manner of life. Also, with an regular dynamic purchaser test of 15 million, Twitch is clearly no longer a social degree you may neglect about.

Twitch started as a facet venture of Justin TV. By 2014, the diploma had extended a splendid variety of supporters. Superbrand, Amazon, saw capability in it and bought it for $340 million. From that point in advance, Twitch has gone from team spirit to first-rate. Twitch is in which content makers can display their competencies, interface with their crowds, fabricate very near networks, and bring in cash doing what they love to do.

Content makers are particular "Streamers" on Twitch. Streamers make channels wherein the whole thing of their streams is located away. As you amplify on the diploma, Twitch opens severa prizes and adapting options. You can improve from a Streamer to Affiliate to Partner. Investigate the most effective-of-a-kind streaming tiers on Twitch:

1. Streamer: Anyone can motion on Twitch, however human beings under 18 years antique want parental assent in advance than going live. Streamers can talk content material material, go to with their crowd, get right of access to their bypass research, and produce collectively a network of fans. As a Streamer, you could start progressing inside the route of becoming a Twitch Affiliate, a status so that it will open severa selective highlights and compensations for you. You can show your improvement via the Achievements internet net page, which you could access underneath Home > Insights > Achievements. When you fulfill the passing tips, you will see a connection

from Twitch welcoming you to locally to be had as an Affiliate.

2. Twitch Affiliate: As a Twitch Affiliate, you can have diverse remarkable apparatuses to be had to you. You'll get a club button on your lovers and a custom act out. If you're endeavoring to get thru from Twitch, you need to accomplish the Affiliate degree. Twitch Affiliates can adapt their directs in severa manners, which consist of:

•Supporters may be blessing you Bits, which may be traded for genuine cash

•Acquire coins with the useful resource of manner of advancing coming near near video video games and selling in-game matters

•Promotions and presents

•Bring in coins from memberships

The base capabilities for turning into an Affiliate embody:

•Reach = 50 devotees

•Broadcast = eight hours or seven days in 30 days

•Normal of 3 traffic for every move (for in any occasion 3 simultaneous streams)

In case you're not kidding about splitting the Affiliate Program, display your achievements through the Achievements internet page.

three. Twitch Partner application: If you're an effective Affiliate, you may pass after the Twitch Partner software, which assurances prepared help and higher-adapting opportunities.

Twitch Partners understand the accompanying benefits:

•Gain month to month memberships

•Confirmed identification for your channel

•Custom identifications for endorsers

•Custom acts out

•Lockable talks which are to be had just for your supporters

•Limited admittance on your substance chronicles

•Incapacitate vending evaluation or supply that manipulate in your endorsers

There are three measures you have to meet for turning into a Partner:

•Time streamed = 25 hours over the maximum present day 30 days

•One of a type days streamed = 12 over the most modern day 30 days

•Normal of seventy five website online visitors for each circulate

After you meet those benchmarks, you may need to fill a proper Partner software for Twitch to don't forget. On the off threat that Twitch supports your software, you'll be an first rate Twitch Partner. We've assembled a word listing of Twitch-common terms for you. Experiencing the ones depictions will assist you in seeing how Twitch abilties.

four.Follows: People who are keen on your streams may also moreover additionally pick out to tail you. On the off hazard that they have set up Twitch warnings, they will be recommended every time you bypass at the web.

five.Talk/ Chat messages: Every steamer gets a go to live with their record. You can deactivate yours in case you want it. In any case, I prescribe which you use the go to to to interface with viewers coordinated.

6.Memberships or subs: Once you are an Affiliate, you can fee a month to month sum from your supporters. Supporters can decide to pay on a one-time or repeating premise. They advantage admittance to your acts out and distinctive blessings characterised with the aid of you.

7.Acts out: Twitch gives a top notch act out a library that can be applied to talk responses even as visiting and streaming. Associates and accomplices may need to make custom acts out.

8.Advertisements: Twitch Partners and Affiliates can run promotions on their channels and produce in cash from them. These are splendid on web page load or mid-flow into, contingent upon your selling settings.

9.Layouts: To deliver your channel an unmistakable look, Twitch permits you to utilize instant codecs. Formats comprise all of the adjustable quantities of your channel, together with forums, overlays, standards, symbols, and alarms.

10. Twitch Extension: You may be a part of expansions from the Twitch Extension Manager into your channel. Utilizing expansions, your endorsers may additionally need to make leaderboards, surveys, and smaller than famous games.

11. Twitch Bits: Subscribers can "Cheer" subsidiaries and accomplices via the usage of sending them Bits through the go to. The slightest bit is as of now pegged at $0.01. You can urge endorsers of utilization Bits for surveying or for celebrating defining moments in your transmission.

12. Merchandise via Amazon: if you're an Amazon account holder and Twitch Partner, you could pursue Merch via Amazon. By doing this, you may gather

each time the custom product is offered for your channel.

How Might You Access Twitch?

To start gushing on Twitch, or to view or statement on streams, you need to make a record on Twitch. You can get to Twitch thru their actual internet internet site or the Twitch software program, which is offered on iOS, Android, Mac, and comfort hobby stations like PS4 and Xbox One. Livestreaming on Twitch is past the world of imagination until you employ unique programming, for instance, OBS and Streamlabs. You will likewise require a respectable nice headset so you can supply analysis and react to comments. When you have got were given all the gadget set up, you can make a profile for your self and start streaming.

While the records show that Twitch houses a top notch deal of gaming content material cloth, you could discover particular styles of the substance furthermore. At the component once I ordered our rundown of the top 30 Twitch streamers, I determined people from numerous backgrounds who're inflicting a ripple effect on the volume. It's a clever concept to do not forget the substance the ones top streamers are sharing to get the cling of the form of substance that prevails at the degree.

Whatever making a decision to movement, tailor it to the necessities and pastimes of the organization. IIf which you need some statistics that will help you with arranging your substance manner for Twitch, right right right here they may be:

•Almost forty one.Five% of Twitch clients are male. That may be ordinary because of the truth that gaming is extra mainstream amongst men than ladies.

•Shockingly, maximum of Twitch customers aren't teenagers and tweens. Mostly, they lie inside the 18-34 years age section.

•Twitch collects a splendid deal of coins for altruistic capabilities. Thus, in case you champion a commendable social reason, you will be a strong healthy for the quantity.

Make tremendous to enjoy Twitch's people employer policies before you start streaming. It consists of preferred prohibitory ideas towards contemptuous and fierce substances, similarly to incredible hints for game enthusiasts and decorations. Live streaming can be energizing really as overwhelming, especially for amateurs. Even even though you could trial your float in advance, you can not be sufficiently organized to address unexpected system faults sooner or later of showtime. You're essentially all on my own as quickly because the digicam starts offevolved rolling. You get the opportunity to reveal your real character, and you want to installation a first rate first connection.

In the wake of searching numerous well-known substance makers, we've got were given assembled a rundown of regulations and regulations that decorations ought to comply with on Twitch.

•Compose guidelines about how visitors need to behave for your channel. Ensure that your policies are unmistakably verified on your web web page.

•Try now not to commandeer discussions with the aid of way of occurring and on or advancing your channel. Offer savvy dialogue and adroit comments.

•Be imaginative for your substance, yet stay regular together with your location of information. This will help you in installing energy and characteristic your capabilities better.

•Attempt to keep institutions with site visitors. Talk and use acts out generously on the identical time as streaming.

•Assemble institutions with similar decorations. Invest power in the suitable networks and look for joint strive openings with different substance makers.

•Never replica the substance of various streamers. You can land in a valid contest that could damage your odds of radiating at the extent.

Regardless of whether or not or no longer you want to interface with game enthusiasts, have eSports worrying conditions, show off your potential, or certainly apprehend high-quality live substance, Twitch is the spot to be. Utilizing the statistics on this content, you can begin your Twitch venture surely.

Chapter 3: Step By Step Guide On How To Earn Money With Twitch

Numerous humans need to live within the realm of digital gaming. Gaming continuously receives a time allotment in their not unusual manner of life, paying little heed to the weight they are experiencing. Anyway, now not the whole lot video video games can be named as "time squandering additives" as there are not many with the useful resource of which you may make a better than not unusual diploma of coins at the same time as stressing your eyes in advance than the display display display screen for pretty a long time. One of the well-known video games is Twitch. Here you may grandstand your gaming potential in advance than one hundred million worldwide clients and might gain attractive cash simultaneously.

Indeed, earlier than reading similarly the overall cycle at the maximum talented method to utilize Twitch as a gaining middle factor, I should to start with come to be more familiar with the sport first. Twitch is a web level that offers the opportunity to newbie and skilled gamers to reveal off their gaming aptitudes to the complete global.

Numerous gamers have been critical for Twitch for years and are gaining endless greenbacks each month. Twitch has very nearly a hundred million site visitors stay on its gateway on a non-save you premise.

There is a part of subjects that you want to supply first earlier than beginning to make a higher than the average salary. In this way, I present to you the essential step by step degree to help you with arriving at a powerful to stage from being a beginner. Ensure you satisfy all the necessities as referenced on the ones way and do a little issue it takes not to bypass, as you could discover hard to comply with returned any mistake by way of evading it.

Step 1: Open A Twitch Account

Above all else, you want to open a twitch account collectively along with your login subtleties. Presently, do no longer spare a second at the same time as pursuing a top charge variation. You can get a portion of the more benefits like facilitates, paid fanatics to speak, and so forth., in case you skip for the pinnacle beauty membership. Note, if you have been talking stay gaming recordings on YouTube, at that point no compelling cause to freeze on the quality way to move all of your recorded recordings to Twitch, with out a copyrights problem. Because of a few interior association, you may flow your report to Twitch, and now not the usage of a hassle. Just those subjects may be authorised which is probably allowed in keeping with the Twitch statistics technique. Now, to move your YouTube record to Twitch, you want to meet the accompanying requirements:

•Over 15,000 perspectives for your gaming communicated recordings.

•You should have extra than 100,000 endorsers.

•Your substance should observe the Twitch expressions of management and DMCA(Digital Millennium Copyright Act)

Step 2: Choose An Appropriate Game

Presently, there are as of now numerous game enthusiasts in Twitch which have their fan base and supporters that pay them to try their nowadays dispatched activity and beautify it for procurement. It can be tough so you can acquire a big style of supporters in a great deal less time. To counter this present, you need to move for those video video games which may be a lot less well-known and are of tons less hobby. This progression might also moreover appear to be slight; but, to stay in Twitch for thinking about that pretty some time within the past run, you need to start with none training. These little games will deliver you a top notch degree of endorsers and in a while, consequently, your supporter's numbers will start to increase. Note, in case you want to pull in more traffic from everywhere in the global, there are numerous gaming intermediaries available through which website site visitors from numerous worldwide locations can watch your live transfer/transferred recordings. First off, you may attempt Lime Proxies, an a-list certifiable middleman worker with fast internet and brief assist, day in and day journey organized for control, and offers a net velocity of over one hundred Mbps with 40+ areas.

Step three: Interaction With Viewers

You can't gain a fan base with out making correspondence with them. There is a preference of go to, close to the gaming zone to your show display display. Ensure, you react for your site visitors' solicitation and tips, with the purpose that they sense remembered for your journey of dominating the healthy. This particular approach can provide you with honest fans, and you could see the range of steadfast enthusiasts developing. So for what purpose to play around on my own whilst you can embody your very non-public "gaming family" for your excursion.

Step four: Apply For Advertisements

In the wake of getting an OK measure of notoriety on Twitch, you'll be licensed to place classified ads among your video games. These promotions might be given to you via the usage of the usage of

Twitch, and the gaining you made thru on the way to be similarly shared among you and Twitch. The installment is probably handled with the useful resource of Twitch in your separate PayPal account. On the off chance that you vicinity commercials of any sport and the viewer taps on it, you could assume a decent cut from it. Additionally, Twitch is possessed through Amazon, so there can be severa classified ads, straightforwardly connected to Amazon game buy. Pick your Ads admirably, as the proper viable motive you to win in a huge kind of bucks. Note, in case you region your marketing previously or among the real-time video, there is a greater prominent risk that they will kill or go away. No one gets a kick out of the hazard to get hindered through way of a few mindless commercials, now not for all, but a few in the middle of interesting minutes in the course of net-based totally completely recordings. In this way, higher spot it toward the end of the video, and do no longer stress; your committed fans will live spherical to have a take a look at your marketing.

Step 5: Become A Sponsor

In the wake of putting in yourself emphatically, you can have a huge quantity of endorsers and viewers. As you emerge as increasingly famous over the extent, you will be selected some of the trivial few, for helping currently dispatched video video games in the marketplace. The gaming enterprise organisation will offer you a super diploma of cash to play this project in your telecom station and lift them to your traffic. Note, you'll be flabbergasted with the style of gaming agencies moving in the direction of you, so if such scenario emerges, enlist an person associate for your budgetary looking after. You would possibly select now not to get hauled into any form of fee troubles, so higher recruit a money associated expert to deal with the a part of the record. The income may be particularly immoderate; this is the cause it's miles proposed to makes this precise stride sincerely.

Step 6: Join In Twitch Accomplice Program

Presently, this is something that may be a big stake for game enthusiasts. The 2d you get mainstream and pull in an massive massive kind of viewers on your channel, you will be supplied a "Twitch accomplice software." Under this software, you will be given the choice to alternate over your site site visitors into endorsers. Presently, you may get an appealing diploma of coins for really getting endorsers, but that sum may be similarly separated many of the telecaster and Twitch. You will collect coins, unbiased of the situation wherein your endorsers do not watch your video. You can likewise begin your promoting attempt, for instance, hand made stock gives and some extra, to boom your income. At this diploma, you are allowed thru Twitch to show off your marketing try and your recordings.

Your supporters can also touch you straightforwardly as they could speak with you in personal, gets complete admittance to your video files, and one-of-a-type scope of emojis to utilize on the identical time as seeing your recordings. They in reality want to shop for on your channel and pay $five every month to take gain of these workplaces.

There are basically three conditions that a telecaster want to need to meet to get the blessings of the Twitch accomplice software application:-

•Getting considerable viewership of 500+ people for your recordings.

•As regularly as feasible, moving and stay actual-time gaming recordings, at any charge, 3 times every week.

•Feature content material material this is excellent underneath the rules of Twitch's group of management and DMCA (Digital Millennium Copyright Act.)

It is a definitive dream for every telecaster on Twitch to enlist themselves inside the Twitch accomplice software program. In this manner, in case you get an opportunity, get it tight. Indeed, this is an odd enhance; however, it's based upon you to tail it or now not.

Step 7: Go For The Donations

If you are to be had, you could request a present to your viewers. You surely want to encompass prepared notices and broadcast stay, so you can display to them approximately the degree of offers you have got become. Attempt to be liberal, amiable, and interesting with the cause that website online traffic will find out you extra as a loosen up person and, on this way, greater offers. You can likewise make a conventional statement approximately the "Gifts of the day" or "The donator of the week" to recognize their help and backing. These sort of bodily sports will maximum probably invite your visitors to provide more. You may need to make a completely particular spot on your channel for the donators, to cause them to enjoy brilliant. You should likewise are looking for recommendation from the set goals that you need to accomplish. Twitch indicates your present very last in an remarkable diagram that furthermore looks as if your budgetary outstanding. As the affords are made, your repute will increment inside the chart. This will motive your traffic to hook up with your goals as their own.

These are more than one steps which might be critical in getting a whole accomplishment in Twitch. Presently, the ones approach have their interesting esteem and may be achieved in reality within the wake of arriving at a particular state of affairs on occurrence degree in Twitch. So do not attempt to exaggerate a few issue; look at your energy, great impulses, and people formerly cited steps to win cash via Twitch.

Ways To Make Money With Twitch

There are subjects about live gushing in 2020 all people have to understand. The first is that stay streaming isn't always quite a great deal gambling laptop games and welcoming others to look at you as you do it; plenty of that prevalence round. The second, and probable greater full-size, is that for some, humans stay streaming is some factor aside from a activity – it's miles a real earnings circulate. A few people can recall it everyday employment.

Be that as it could, do now not prevent yours yet. The statistics verify that it is unbelievably clean to begin live streaming. It's moreover obvious that some humans understand the way to hold in coins streaming, and there is no motivation inside the again of why you probable may not figure out how to do it, as well. You may furthermore without a doubt have the choice to take in a few matters from corporations which is probably utilising it – that is how inescapable stay streaming has come to be.

On Twitch, the precept five,000 channels get 75% of all survey time. Arriving at in which you almost receives a commission to stay movement calls for splendid funding, electricity, and that particular a few issue as a way to make people want to look at you. The individuals who are getting rich streaming are unfathomably little minority. On Twitch, as an instance, the number one 5,000 channels get seventy five% of all survey time. Twitch has over 2,000,000 channels. In case you're organized to vicinity inside the artwork into bringing in coins via live streaming, put together.

Ways You Can Make Money Live Streaming

Here are probably the most famous, hassle unfastened techniques to do it, trailed via the usage of those that require greater inclusion or are truly exceptional.

1.Getting gives or pointers from enthusiasts

If you're searching for proof that your stay video actual-time facet interest/facet gig/profession is shifting a high-quality way, the main present or a tip is a excellent one. You'll get a sincerely unusual inclination whilst it takes vicinity to you that everybody, somewhere, is acknowledging what you are doing what is had to supply you numerous greenbacks. Most stay-streaming tiers and internet websites can help you deliver in coins spilling with the aid of letting web site traffic send you gives or hints. They typically have coordinated administrations, or maybe their personal "digital merchandise" or "monetary bureaucracy" traffic can use for the exchange.

Here's a breakdown of what a part of the vast degrees uses:

•YouTube's principle tipping manage is Super Chat. Viewers can make use of recommendations to stick messages on your channel's go to window, making them more observable. YouTube likewise we could clients buy visit movements known as Super Stickers, and you get a lessen of each buy.

•Twitch lets in visitors to "cheer" making use of Bits, the degree's digital appropriate. In case you're a Twitch subsidiary or an companion, you get spherical a penny for every Bit viewer's use on the equal time as cheering. The traffic get the possibility to compose a message that indicates up in conjunction with an great shape of act out, a Cheemote.

•Facebook's tipping management spins round Stars, a kind of outstanding virtual website online traffic should buy and deliver to you, providing you with a penny for every Star. You ought to be an component of Facebook's Level Up utility to empower Stars. Facebook additionally underpins elevating coins magnanimous gives for a U.S.- based.

•The Mixer has a framework wherein site traffic acquire Sparks with the resource of looking streams and spend them on Skills — liveliness and gifs. Getting Skills will have you ever ever a payout. Viewers can likewise buy Embers and alternate them for extra extremely good Skills, which get you extra payouts.

•DLive we may want to viewers make blockchain-primarily based truly Lino focuses with the aid of manner of using connecting with individuals' streams. They can ship the ones focuses to you as a blessing.

Most stay-streaming stages and websites can help you supply in cash gushing with the aid of manner of letting visitors ship you items or suggestions. When getting pointers, ensure to provide a holler to the character giving it. On the off threat that the end accompanies a message or an inquiry throughout a live AMA, it would be a smart notion to arrange it over regular inquiries for solutions.

2.Normal viewer installments on the streaming diploma

What's better than getting a periodic tip from your viewers? Getting a fashionable installment. These substantial installments commonly net you a couple of dollars every, however if you may get enough of them, they sure can encompass. You generally need to meet wonderful conditions for empowering this sort of help, as ranges store it for human beings from their substance dressmaker applications. The stages that don't have it but will possibly function out this element later on, because it's carrying out being a mainstream approach to usher in cash streaming—large viewer installments on the streaming degree.

Here's the way part of the degrees is dealing with this:

•YouTube has a channel participation application that permits clients to get channels collectively with often scheduled installments. To open your channel to this chance, you want to be inside the YouTube Partner Program and meet extra qualification situations.

•Twitch has a paid club software program that we could you got from paid memberships if you're an Affiliate or Partner. Your visitors get one membership for no longer a few element through Twitch Prime, or they are able to pay for them the usage of PayPal, Amazon Pay, or Mastercards.

•Facebook Gaming has a membership utility underway.

•The Mixer has a Partner Payments software with memberships, letting clients set up installments with playing cards or PayPal.

If the degree you operate allows it, you want to make content this is reachable only for your supporters. This is a pleasant method to offer your maximum steadfast website online site visitors noticeably greater for their assist. Additionally, ensure to present a holler to the people who bought in, and in all likelihood supply them a phrase on their membership commemoration.

three. Tips and not unusual installments thru outsider tiers

You likely may not want all your streaming earnings to experience the streaming degree. Dislike all and sundry must be too eager on becoming a member of the commercial enterprise enterprise packages, for example. You may moreover likewise worry what occurs if you lose your popularity and your last with the stage. Perhaps you definitely need to keep matters separate to make it less complicated to move to start with one platform, then onto the other, or work on a few stages simultaneously.

•Begin multistreaming today.

•Contact a more good sized crowd thru gushing to numerous ranges all of the whilst.

•Out of the blue, you may grow to be in need of an intruder degree you can use to deal with gives and memberships. There's bounty you could appearance over. The absolute maximum well-known alternatives encompass:

•Streamlabs for one-time gadgets. It includes successfully with Twitch, YouTube, Mixer, Facebook, Periscope, and Picarto, and it gives six numerous installment options.

•Patreon for everyday presents/memberships. With its potential to allow supporters set month to month vows, Patreon is about the closest problem you may get to the club framework degrees are regularly receiving.

•GoFundMe or Kickstarter for task based financing. If you have were given were given an project you could determine upon to complete, and you're searching out financing, installation pages on those internet web sites and employ your stay streams to growth your challenge.

For a aspect of these administrations, if not maximum, you may must recall making splendid rewards and substance for those who uphold you. Be cautious while selecting what is going within the returned of the paywall and what stays a part of your middle – and loose – content, but. You cannot hold all your fantastic stuff in the lower back of the divider.

Some of it wants to stay allowed to tug in new traffic.

four.Income from promotions

Why now not use promotions to help your stay streaming? Publicizing bucks are, as of now, used to govern a massive part of the internet, together with Google administrations and Facebook. If you be part of the nice streaming stage or interpersonal enterprise employer, you can start gaining the publicizing cash, as properly.

You will in reality need to join the precise streaming degree, but, due to the truth now not every considered one of them gives advertisements. Some are decided enemies of promotions, for instance, DLive. Others, as an instance, Mixer, for example, host now not but integrated a third-get-together selling control.

If commercials are what you want to usher in cash from, these are the tiers to enroll in:

•YouTube gives pre-roll and mid-glide advertisements, certainly as show and overlay promotions.

•Facebook Live gives mid-glide classified ads in case you meet the viewership extensive range models.

•Twitch gives in-flow into promotions, simply as show and nearby commercial openings.

Promoting stay streaming is an exciting hassle and an ordinary reason for debate. You need to exercise as masses control as feasible over the classified ads proven in some unspecified time inside the future of your streams or in your channel. Additionally, hold in thoughts that visitors can employ commercial impeding programming to maintain a few promotions from performing. It's now not the nice plan to have commercials because the best model choice in your stay streaming.

5.Brand preparations and sponsorships

Less disputable than everyday advertisements, logo preparations, and sponsorships are each one-of-a-kind manner you may draw in with businesses in a typically useful plan. If that you have a big after on streaming tiers and you've got got emerge as well-known, producers will touch you with gives. On the off danger that they do not, you could want to do the connecting. In any case, whilst dealing with producers, it could pay to be proficient and conscientious. You'll need to set up the details of the association, to be 100% awesome you are in the identical spot concerning your obligation.

Manners in which you supply in cash gushing thru preparations with manufacturers embody:

•Sponsorships, wherein your complete streams are supported through way of a logo.

•Standards and specific varieties of commercials you can show inside the path of your streams or for your channel or profile page at the level.

•Supported substance, much like at the same time as a recreation engineer pays you to play their undertaking.

Your crowd is the element to be able to stand out sufficient to be noticed. Twitch moreover offers an preference to hold your identity solid and hide from the employer that could create problem for you. The association you strike is the way you deliver in coins streaming. Simply be conscious so as no longer to do deals if you want to motive you to expose up as a sellout. Your crowds in all likelihood may not that way, and on the off hazard that you lose them, you lose the assist.

Build a worthwhile Twitch target market

Building a live streaming crowd can be dubious. Here are a few live streaming tips to boom your opportunity for progress. With YouTube commercials carried out giving the profits, they as soon as did, severa gamers have long long past to stay to move. It thoroughly may be doubtful approximately assembling and preserving a live streaming crowd. Considering that, proper right right here are some live streaming hints to allow your channel to succeed.

1.Discover Games That Are Trending

When deciding on video games for live movement, you will need to select new and well-known video video games which can be as of now standing out. Moving video video games are certain to get the eye of site visitors, helping them discover your channel. Check the extremely good gaming destinations and net crawlers to appearance which ongoing games are in the information and earning acclaim from gamers. If you may find out the pre-discharge duplicate of a particular mainstream activity, that may be a protracted way and away advanced.

Are you searching out the amazing laptop exercise records internet web site and challenge survey places? These believed gaming places provide remarkable inclusion of a full-size style of pc video games. The Twitch landing page moreover shows a rundown of well-known video games among visitors if you're combating to discover thoughts. In any case, it's far consistently turning into to do your exam at the off threat that you in reality need to find out what the gaming network is at gift zeroing in on.

Simultaneously, you may choose not to pick video video video games that, as of now, have oversaturated inclusion. Some mainstream games will, at present, have decorations protecting them months or years after dispatch. It's hard to rival intensely settled streams that have secured unique video video games for an brilliant time. Crowds of AAA titles with oversaturated inclusion will, in sizable, adhere to the decorations they recognize, as they've had considerable possibilities to discover who spreads games such that they admire. In this manner, you want to make a decision new out of doors the arena titles which might be much less contemporary-day, however although mainstream.

2.Live Stream Games Consistently

Similarly, as with this form of substance dishing out, you want to hold a everyday timetable while beginning a streaming channel. You can alter this timetable depending upon it gradual obligations; however, consistency is vital. You want to maintain a regular, preferred yield in region of gushing in blasts and in some time going quiet for capricious timeframes. If which you do not have a whole lot of time at some stage inside the week, do not try to movement each day. It's smarter to circulate as soon as according to week or actually at the ends of the week, in that case. Crowds lean toward consistency over sporadic and unpredictable substance plans.

three.Prop The Conversation Up

If you really take a seat quietly even as gambling your pastime on a stay circulation, there is a sorry cause at the back of others to look at you. Try no longer to strain: you won't want to continuously speak, mainly if your interest requires center. Notwithstanding, keeping a communicate streaming goes some distance in maintaining your crowd locked in. In an data escalated exercising or jail, make clear your approach and what you're doing. When playing an easygoing recreation, declaration to your initial introductions.

On the off threat that you've clearly finished this, communicate with your visitors, who will likely positioned up questions and comments within the go to phase. It should not all want to be recognized with the game - at times, your crowd honestly wants to emerge as acquainted with you. The type of discussions you have will likewise rely upon your crowd. For example, endorsers of the unique Yogscast live streams often make the maximum of their extraneous humor. A organization of humans of horrific-to-the-bone game enthusiasts can also want more path and suggestions on the subject of difficult video games.

four.Express Gratitude Toward New Subscribers On Your Stream

Endorsers on recreation streaming locales, as an example, Twitch, are your meat and potatoes, so that you must explicit gratitude towards them in like manner. Indeed, even a touch willpower reasons you to bring in cash from gaming, so make certain your crowd realizes that you fee it. This might be tough to do at the same time as you're looking to zero in on a recreation; but, you may make use of a streaming module to quite mechanize the cycle. You have to pay attention to this does not supplant the want to make an character word in some unspecified time in the future of your float. Yet, it gives them a few acknowledgment even as you hang tight for a hollow on your ongoing interplay in which you can bypass your consideration.

five.Take Game And Song Requests

This is each one-of-a-kind approach to reveal your crowd that you care about their facts and exams. During your float, ask them which video games they will need you to move after your subsequent meeting. If you like to play tunes sooner or later of your circulate, you could likewise take needs. The primary offer of allowing crowd people to pick a tune in your playlist is going some distance in encouraging conversation.

6.Interface With Your Followers On Social Media

Discussing cooperation, a part of your crowd individuals will want to interface with you outdoor of motion speak. This is specially obvious in the occasion that they can not tune in without fail. You need to share your unique public net-primarily based definitely media handles alongside facet your supporters. No, you do no longer want to end up Facebook companions with every devotee. In any case, you may percentage your Twitter deal with and a few exceptional internet-based media pages that you need them to go to.

Regardless of whether you're no longer sharing gaming-related posts, severa crowd humans will, in any case, be keen on what you need to nation. You can also even take a look at casual companies which might be explicitly for gamers. The huge concept is to hook up with your crowd outdoor of streaming meetings.

7.Give The Audience Incentives To Return

Progressively, crowd human beings are eager to buy in to or guide content material cloth makers who provide them the right motivations. Live to motion, notwithstanding, is marginally no longer similar to fashionable substance advent.

Probably the right method to do this is using giveaways. Simply make certain which you realize the necessities round demanding situations for the degree you're the usage of, and the locale you are taking walks the competition in. Extraordinary mind for giveaways are present vouchers, enterprise assist memberships, and video games. Things like the ones, which you may deliver keys for cautiously, can spare you dispatching charges at the same time as you're surely starting. Contingent upon your streaming stage, you may have the selection to beautify memberships.

For instance, Twitch offers endorser truly streams. As your channel develops, you can component better or even get supported prizes from precise businesses. However, if you're as but an newbie, you may probable discover a few gaming arrangements to component with.

8.Get A Sponsor For Your Live Stream

For this improvement, you need to, as of now, have pretty of an after. Notwithstanding, getting help assist you to in developing your crowd similarly. Getting assistance is often referred to via decorations as a way of developing a larger after. Some developments this to the extended believability that accompanies being embraced via a emblem.

If you cannot find out manual in the meanwhile, you need to awareness on partner repute on a level like Twitch. This builds your validity at the same time as presenting you with extra profits streams. Notwithstanding, this takes big tough work and isn't always a handy guide a rough solution for growing an after.

9.Get Other Gamers Involved

While live streaming is often a usual performance adventure, it's miles high-quality to get some one in each of a type game enthusiasts engaged together with your streams. It couldn't need to be a cutting-edge element or an brilliant business enterprise. Be that as it could, an intermittent collection may be an wonderful expansion on your channel.

Attempt to discover gamers with whom you have got got a few technological understanding. Exchange is one of the most appealing things for gaming crowds, in particular in multiplayer video video games. You won't want the gamer to show up head to head. Indeed, some tremendous institutions are formed between decorations which have in no way met disconnected.

You can likewise display up on some other man or woman's circulate, with a purpose to give you a further presentation to potential new crowd human beings. Crew Stream we could Twitch decorations broadcast together.

10. Utilize Decent Equipment

One crucial interest that influences your crowd's evaluation revel in is streaming brilliant. You do now not have to strain over building up an immaculate, 4K go with the flow. In any case, you need to make certain the first rate is exceptional. Murmuring mouthpieces, genuine package deal misfortune, and profoundly pixelated visuals will pursue most crowds away. Make a aspect to outfit your self with an exceptional amplifier and a brief net affiliation in advance than you flow. If you want to see your flow into, located sources into an OK webcam as well. Likewise, do not try to play around, which may be excessively excessive for your gaming rig.

Live streaming can be an unbelievably compensating enjoy. In case you are geared up to make a streamable substance from some thing you need doing, you may earnings via beginning to waft. Regardless of whether or no longer or no longer it is through making new partners, finding new enterprise openings, or simply running toward your exhibition skills, streaming can surely benefit you. To the volume places wherein you could talk attractive substance bypass, Twitch is an simple pinnacle preference. It's the precept diploma that is correctly making its approaches for a big type of materials, from gaming to ASMR and entire-frame cosmetics academic wearing activities. The degree is so mainstream and large in the marketplace that identifying the way to transport to Twitch may be very almost a transitional revel in for future substance makers.

Be that as it is able to, Twitch isn't the principle diploma reachable. A extremely good part of the exhortation you have to follow even as spilling to Twitch likewise applies to super ranges. By identifying the manner to be an powerful ornament on Twitch, you could become acquainted with a few topics that could assist you with blossoming with precise stages, as well. In case you're looking for an method to unfold your substance over a few tiers, Restream is the device you ought to make use of.

Especially as a streaming learner, it has a bent to be useful to be available on a few degrees all of the while. Along these strains, you may increase your variety and the full-size form of adherents.

This sounds sensible from the outset. However, it isn't viable to widely recognized it with Twitch, because of the fact there can be a proviso inside the phrases and conditions that disallows concurrent spilling on Twitch and specific tiers even as you are an partner or companion of Twitch. Because of the way that the member repute is done fairly abruptly and efficiently, you can, first rate case situation, overlook approximately it right away, because it brings more exertion than an advantage. Should you need to provide streaming a shot severa degrees toward the begin, there's uncommon multistream programming available to help you with placing your association with out hesitation. The most well-known is the free programming restream. There will now not be a chance to figure out a way to motion to Twitch. The Amazon-claimed live-streaming stage is host to greater than 2 million telecasters who circulate to endless traffic a month. What's greater, it is some thing past an opening to play and watch games — Twitch streams presently comprise everything from large stage Call of Duty pastime to cooking shows and unrecorded tune.

Even better, all and sundry may be a Twitch ornament. You can float live proper out of your cell cellphone or help in case you really need to attempt matters out, and in case you want to gather a extra covered advent from your PC or Mac, all you want is a few free programming and more than one bits of rigging to begin.

•Some satisfactory gaming PCs are first-rate for streaming

•There are a few quality webcams for talking collectively together with your crowd

In case you are fortunate, you may even supply in some coins from streaming gratitude to Twitch's Affiliate and Partner programs. So whether or not or not you're searching for to assess spilling for no particular motive or need to encourage your excursion to Twitch superstardom, proper right here's all that you need to understand for a manner to movement to Twitch.

There are one-of-a-kind selections, as properly. If you need to build up coins from gaming, you could likewise keep in mind turning into an engineer, or maybe a pundit. You can instruct, you can compose books… There are pretty some strategies to convert your enthusiasm right right right into a vocation.

Chapter 4: Step By Step Guide To Starting Streaming On Twitch

Twitch, Amazon's stay-streaming platform, has greater than 2 million broadcasters broadcasting to hundreds and thousands and thousands of visitors monthly. There has never been a time whilst people have found out to transport on Twitch. Twitch Streams now have the whole thing from a high diploma of Call of Duty motion to cooking indicates and stay song. And it is no longer simply a place for looking and playing video video games.

Now, you, I, and each person may be a broadcaster on Twitch. You can pass stay proper far from your console or cellphone so long as you need to test the water, and if you need to mix the most involved product to your PC or Mac, all you need is loose software program and a few quantities more add-ons to get started out out.

If you're into gambling video video games on Twitch and spend many hours a day looking games as properly, you could start something interesting in your existence by manner of using turning into a streamer. This streaming platform is gaining recognition these days, and if you aren't the usage of it, you are missing out on some element thrilling however vital. Its siren songs are almost hard to pass. If you're inquisitive about the usage of Twitch and do not realize a manner to, this manual could be clearly useful. There is lots to understand approximately in advance than you start streaming, and additionally the technical element appears overwhelming. Not only do you require the Hardware to play the game, but all the special vital competencies and boundaries to make your streaming live on Twitch. Without breaking the financial group, you may do exceptional streaming if you have the right mixture of system. There is the primary statistics you need to have at the same time as you get started out, however you don't have to interrupt the financial organization for that. Here, the budgeting can be an problem, mainly for loads hobbyists, so if you have to pick out the maximum crucial ones and save the others for later, you need to don't forget the following:

•A tool through which you could make a connection

•A constant and strong Internet connection for broadcasting

•Software to help you movement.

•Some useful devices Audio and visible

You can circulation song, paintings, activity, or every different sports sports movement with a few steps below:

Step 1 Prepare for streaming on Twitch

Well, the clean manner out is you can visit Twitch sincerely, create an account there, and begin streaming. Although probably, you may now not be capable of acquire many visitors this way. You have to give you some aspect really well worth highlighting as, on Twitch, there are extra than 7 million channels. Before you begin working on Hardware, streaming software software program, and one-of-a-kind add-ons, it's miles crucial to build up essential records, so that you do no longer turn out to be wasting time there.

Step 2 Review Terms of Services and the Community Guidelines

It is the most crucial step. It is continually endorsed to set your Balance and Safety settings in advance than the number one broadcast to ensure you and your network get to have the excellent feasible experience. You must go through the Community Guidelines for the pink streaming platform in advance than even taking step one on Twitch. It might be very essential to understand what your limits are, what you may and can not do. For example, racism, hate speech, discrimination toward site visitors, or unlicensed recording track isn't allowed. There is also direct mail to control, get dressed codes to examine, and one-of-a-kind critical elements.

If the number one topics referred to appear to you on the equal time as you're offline, Twitch will nevertheless artwork for your channel. Messages additionally may be said from other traffic. It is, consequently, critical that your Twitch channel is greater regular day and night time.

As you cannot be there, 24/7. But it is why there are AutoMods, which help you get out all through AFK time. Note that there you're in reality chargeable for the content cloth of your flow into and all related content material fabric. If you fail to accumulate your responsibilities, it'll bring about consequences. In the worst-case state of affairs, your channel may be clearly banned from the platform. Luckily, it's far very smooth to live away in opposition to this. So observe the Community Guidelines and find out what you need to be aware about.

Step three Create an account

First, you'll need to create a Twitch account in case you do no longer have it already. Turn on Two-Factor Verification to maintain your account steady. Downloading the Twitch app to your iOS or Android device is notably endorsed. You can use it to view streams anywhere, however you could also get right of entry to your creator dashboard to alternate number one settings, play commercials, and be stay.

Step 4 Customize your channel

To allow the trendy traffic, understand who you are where to find out you personalize your channel. With your cellular tool, you may modify your profile photo and bio or, with an internet browser, personalize many extra settings. You can customize your internet page and your channel to mirror you and your product.

Step five Selecting Hardware

It subjects the maximum on which tool you play your activity on. Adjust your setup! You will need to check what Hardware you may need to transport your audio and visuals. You do no longer ought to make subjects difficult. If you private a Play station or Xbox, you could bypass live in only some mins.

Step 6 Selecting Software

Select and installation your streaming software application to get your content fabric available! Twitch Studio is software application application available for Windows and Mac. Both are Twitch's best software application that makes it easy to set up streaming and move stay in most effective mins. Onboard guiding permits to routinely discover your microphone, webcam, and other streaming era functions, and pre-loaded startups assist creators simplify the arrival of the movement. Built-in signs and conversations are there, assisting you without problems view channel hobby and have interaction along facet your community.

Step 7 Plan your circulate

 Plan your broadcast hours and circulate stay now; you are prepared to live, simply go through in thoughts to go into a call, categorize it, and tag the movement so visitors can locate you!

The aspect is simple: If you plan your movement hours, your visitors can time desk their visits to your bypass. It won't assist your fans in case you normally begin streaming robotically on every occasion you revel in adore it. For the 1/three time in some time, while considered one in all your fans misses your drift due to the fact he time and again has no time for you, he's going to be lengthy past no matter how masses he likes you. So, in this case, do not give up and create a schedule it surely is snug together along with your daily life. For instance, you could movement each week after art work and on Saturday that 10 a.M. Whatever your plan, it's going to simplest make sense if others understand it already. You can announce it on Twitch panels and social media. Your fanatics are much more likely to concentrate it proper right here.

Step 8 Get your USP

To stand out from the relaxation, USP is one of the most crucial methods. USP stands for Unique Selling Proposition. To provide an cause of it to you, you may give you many ideas; there are not any limits to your ingenuity. Alternatively, it could be a seen exchange for you; it can be a cover-up.

Decoration, Wig, or the equal. Or other sports related to the video games you play that humans want to take a look at, together with competitions together collectively together with your friends on Apex or Valorant, the ones are exceptional positioned on Twitch. You can also cut up your game content material cloth with small cooking shows or one of a kind recreational sports. Whatever you come across as your USP, recollect that it need to be slightly aligned with some of your content cloth cloth. Be legitimate on Twitch. If site visitors dislike you or the manner you have interaction with them, all the visual refinement, USP, or proper talents in the sport will not assist. Just be yourself. Don't faux it the least bit. That's even as the expertise of "each person receives the right audience" starts offevolved to paintings over and over over again as irrespective of some thing you are; there'll constantly be sufficient humans spherical you who get keep of you as you are.

Step 9 Use overlays to Engage collectively along side your visitors

Many new broadcasters undermine communique with their viewers. You want to set and comply with the rules generally. Otherwise, your chat will speedy fall from your palms. If this is your base, you may create a pleasing communication with your goal market and lovers on it. This consists of frequently greeting new traffic when they be part of a communique. When you study the terms aloud, you have to no longer overreact, in view that there are usually visitors who use the so-referred to as "bait terms." These are a few important phrases which you want to apply in satisfactory a modified shape and have to no longer be marketed greater often live in a talk. Besides, you have to ensure which you maintain the communication alive with the useful resource of the use of posting articles again and again once more. Also, anecdotes or reminiscences are generally welcome out of your lifestyles. This is taken into consideration crucial on the starting whilst there are only a few traffic. Later, the chat becomes greater independent, that is wherein the mods begin to art work, but most of all, it's far predicated upon for your ongoing communication with the web page traffic. Although you may not be able to respond to each message, no reaction isn't an option. This makes you appearance remoted and remote. Also, Twitch gives many abilities that assist you to interact together with your viewers. For example, polls in emotes or communique.

Step 10 Add signals on your movement

Alerts are like an overlay; they increase the circulate. Alerts are to will let you understand at the same time as a person follows you or leaves a subscription to a float. This we must one-of-a-type visitors to do the same and will increase the amount of leisure. Alerts are images that you can combine consequences with OBS and others. Add sounds to them, and you could have double the a laugh. Play tune within the Background. Music can mild up the Background, just like what you examine in a film. Be cautious even as gambling it as any song this is hateful, racist, or biased, and unlicensed is recognized with the aid of manner of Twitch and may ban your account. So, if you need to preserve your Twitch typical ordinary performance, use most effective song this is authorised at the platform and licensed. If you install "Twitch Music" on Google, you could locate many internet websites to help you. Alternatively, use the proper extensions, which you may find on your account.

Chapter 5: Creating A Twitch Account For Live Streaming

When you be a part of up for the account please realise that you conform to the Terms of Service and Privacy Policy further to being held to the Community Guidelines. When you create an account on Twitch it helps you to interact with broadcasters and one among a kind people even as you chat with them, follow your chosen streamers to get notified even as they come to live, and most significantly glide to the Twitch network to your channel. When growing the account, please double-test the details provided before finishing your registration. Accounts placed to be infringing may be fined, collectively with account suspension. If you every so often lose get right of entry to for your account and want to undertake an account healing technique, having correct statistics will appreciably help in that device.

Create an account

Now that you're aware about the community hints, you're geared up to start. First take a look at in on Twitch. Like specific systems, you want to create an account with an e mail address and password. For this, both use your pc or go to Twitch.Tv Tap "Register" After that, a shape can be opened for you to complete. You begin with a username, it's miles the first obstacle to take while inside the flow. The username is the best acting later on your channel's net web page. It's the call your fans will factor to, and it makes the price of popularity. When you will pick out a username, make it to be readable, accessible, now not a random string of characters and, has a effective ring on it. Also, it's miles a terrific idea to test the decision on social media and to ensure that it's miles to be had proper away to keep away from problems over time.

The precise statistics: you can change your name if you want to inside the Twitch settings. Note that this can most effective display up each 60 days. You can exchange the sensitivity of your selected username at any time. Click on "Register" after coming into the email cope with, date of starting, and password on the shape. Confirm your electronic mail via the use of checking your Twitch electronic mail to your inbox and entering the code in the Twitch.Tv form. You want to set -aspect authentication at the "Security and Privacy" tab of your settings to protect your account from unauthorized get admission to. Each time you check in, irrespective of from which device, you can gather a code in your mobile mobile phone or Authy (cellular app). You can sign up satisfactory with this code after entering into your e mail deal with and password. Now, your Twitch account has visible daylight hours. You can start setting and designing your Twitch profile now.

Desktop Signup

Go to the Twitch net web page and join up for the account, and select the signup button at the web web page.

This opens the login alternative/login show display. Fill out the Signup form and be a part of up for a present day account on Twitch.

Choose a username (four-25 characters lengthy), set password, electronic mail, and birthday, and don't forget to inform them you are now not a robotic!

Twitch has were given powerful measures in region to prevent and retrieve money owed created for harassment, the usage of abusive, hateful, or threatening names on usernames. If any username is located in violating the Community Guidelines or the account is found to be created to harass, Twitch at once suspends the account and uses superb hints and appropriate results to guard offerings and the general public.

Mobile signup

To be a part of up for a cellular account, download the Twitch Mobile App to your device. Once you've got downloaded and installed, release the app for your tool and tap the join up button. When you sign on for a mobile account you will be able to join up by means of the usage of the usage of your telephone amount (VOIP smartphone numbers or landline will not be common) or e-mail address. It is frequently recommended to sign up for up along with your cellphone large variety and furthermore upload and affirm your electronic mail to your account sometimes.

Further verify your e-mail deal with to:

Allow sending channel notifications which you examine (if you've enabled notifications).

Allow recuperation of account in case you lose get admission to to your smartphone.

Allows you to talk with channels with confirmed email settings.

Your cellular telephone also can furthermore offer a brief dial opportunity in your cellphone range at the identical time as you're registering which you can use to go into your cellphone range immediately. If you want to use electronic mail alternatively, click on on on Use Email possibility as opposed to an desire further to a brief fill.

Be outstanding to enter your u.S. Code at the same time as registering your telephone variety. Many phones automatically upload the us of the usa code but double-take a look at or there may be a risk you can now not be able to get maintain of messages to verify your massive variety. SMS and records charges may practice right right here.

After finishing the Signup form, click on on the Signup button below. There your cellular phone significant range or e mail deal with might be demonstrated via sending a 6-digit code known as one-time password (OTP) through SMS or e mail.

Some gadgets can robotically fill within the code once you have were given acquired an SMS if you signed up thru cellphone variety. You will want to gather the 6-digit code in SMS or e-mail and installation it in the app interior five mins if your mobile smartphone does no longer help this.

 If you've got got signed up with a tested cell smartphone amount however have not furnished an e mail deal with, important account information thru SMS notifications can be despatched. This is finished to ensure to tell you of things like your account movement. If you now not need to acquire SMS notifications you could reply to STOP at any time and there might be no notifications until you select out to restart. If you do not get maintain of e mail or textual content inside five minutes, on the pinnacle left tap the arrow to go again and check the e-mail and contact amount you supplied and attempt all over again.

If you would love to enter an electronic mail address whilst you sign on using your cell telephone variety, I fantastically advocate getting into your email cope with because it will provide you with some different manner to get higher if you lose get right of access to to your account.

Creating greater bills

Additional Twitch debts can be created anywhere any time provided you take a look at the Terms of Service and Community Guidelines. When you affirm an e-mail deal with to your account, extra creation of money owed with that e-mail deal with is disabled to save you abusive behavior. As a examined email person, for your account you will want to allow settings options inside the protection settings to create extra Twitch bills; unlocking this may can help you be part of up for one extra account.

Please be conscious: Each time you need to sign up for up a further account you could need to re-allow this setting, in reaction to effectively registering the modern-day day account at your installed e-mail cope with will disable similarly processing.

Create a Twitch profile

To make one or greater important settings for your new account, click on on proper to the unfinished profile image and then "Settings". Here you begin through importing a banner and your profile image. If you do now not any of them proper now, you'll locate an entire lot of banners and profile pix on-line. Decide if you could upload your profile image. If no longer you can make a brand as well. Create an avatar that expresses you as an instance in a manga fashion. You can create your Avatar in a few minutes via using any Avatar Maker on-line. However, it's miles very critical to bear the following matters in thoughts.

All designed functions like logo, banner, signs, overlays, and so forth need to be graphically illustrated. In this way, the consistent appearance of your channel is ensured which displays your understanding, professionalism, and draws potential lovers. With many on-line shops extending their assist on line help, you may without troubles get it accomplished. The online help is to be had to you day and night time time whenever you need to get it completed.

After posting a banner and profile image, you could describe your self in some inspiring phrases that could permit others test you in the long term. Be actual right here, you can't be faux as humans gets to recognize as speedy you'll start streaming. Do this all inside the "Biography" phase, which you may find out beneath your username underneath the banner upload. Here you do no longer want to sound too progressive, powerful, or humorous.

For biography, you want to provide your traffic with the maximum actual statistics and that they have to get the effect and idea concerning who you are and what your channel is all about, and what they must assume from your Twitch channel. Remember to put in writing down it all concisely, nobody loves to observe long information. You need to try expressing your self concisely in the awesome viable phrases leaving an eternal have an impact on on people.

Separate chat hints

To keep away from troubles, arguments, foul language, and unique undesirable situations, it's far encouraged to set regulations of communication from the start. Additionally, you have got had been given the possibility to use AutoMod to delete hyperlinks and unique words right now from the communique and to day out the person sending those for a advantageous length. Once you have got achieved all this is required below the 'Profile' tab, you have to get privy to your streaming key.

This key is probably required to get began out collectively with your glide on Twitch and combine out of doors software. To find your waft key you have to click on on the "Channel and motion photographs" section. The first factor you will be conscious is the "Key Stream Key", along facet the enter trouble with various dots, including a password vicinity.

The reality that the posted key modified into made nameless at the beginning is for a super purpose. It is as vital because the password is, and permits you to get entry to to your Twitch account. Anyone who has this key can flow into it thru your channel. So by no means display it on broadcast or some other vicinity. Only you are the handiest who desires the flow into key and no individual else.

Chapter 6: Which Software Should Be Used For Live Streaming?

Hardware, software program application software, and accessories are all which you want to begin streaming. Once they all are ready you may get began. Firstly, the software program is the most crucial component to endure in mind. I will now be running on software application to be able to permit you to flow your show content live at the Internet and display your recreation on Twitch in superb slight.

Like in all different elements of existence, there are lots many software program application that you may use for streaming software software program. Depend on folks that they need to apply because the selections are lots. Four fantastic solutions are right here to provide you with a pinnacle stage view of the streaming software program. Although Twitch additionally gives software program robotically, it has not been carried out however. For this reason, it is better first of all the first-rate proper software program program software program proper from the begin. By this, you could reduce down on severa pressure, and moreover you can not want to alternate the software software application in the destiny.

OBS-Studio

Open Broadcaster Software (OBS) is the oldest of its type. It modified into launched in 2012 and has been the number one company considering the fact that then. It is free software program program and can be accessed through the use of every person the usage of Windows, macOS, or Linux and moreover freed from charge. The functionality of the software program utility is simple to apply, works notable for non-specialists as properly, and if questions stand up or misunderstandings, YouTube has a whole lot of tutorials that offer you with all the solutions.

In addition to streaming feasibly streaming on Twitch, YouTube, and unique structures, OBS moreover permits you to create an smooth recording. For instance, in area of Streaming, you need to create a easy YouTube video. With many settings options, Broadcaster software may be optimized to healthy Hardware and your necessities as properly. You also can create plenty of scenes in order to permit you to function overlays, collectively with loads of many things.

Streamlabs OBS

OBS-Studio is simplest made in partnership with Logitech. From the most well-known house among gamers is Streamlabs, especially designed to manual streamers. Broadcasting is one thing, feeding the human beings with the whole lot you need and disturbing for it's miles each other. Streamlabs OBS combines each efficiently and simply. You can also customise your twitch channel by way of the use of coping with the twitch panels with Streamlabs. Features which encompass more than one widgets, Cloudboy, installing area your signs, and organizing your services are blanketed in the Streamlabs OBS portfolio. In a nutshell: You get the whole thing from one supply, continuously have all the view and make the maximum crucial features are to be had freed from fee.

vMix

This is the software program application that works handiest on Windows but makes complete use of this software. It is based totally on Direct3D, vMix mechanically gets its property from the CPU and GPU.

Therefore, this streaming software program program can reduce delays and transmit first rate Streaming. However, as it's miles a imaginative and prescient mixer software application, vMix specializes in video manufacturing, Streaming, and recording content material material. Functions like Streamlabs aren't able to find proper right here. Over and over again, you get a entire bundle of streaming software program application that you can customize therefore in element for video and audio each. And in the end, remember and not overlook approximately that vMix is no longer free like others. This broadcast software program application best offers a trial version for 60-days.

Xsplit

Xsplit is a fantastic software program application software that is more famous than Streamlabs OBS. It additionally works as an OBS but differs drastically from the man or woman interface. The reality is that you create scenes that you could personalize, regulate your sound, and create exceptional settings that beautify the general streaming revel in.

What makes Xsplit top notch from a wide sort of software program options are that there are exercising broadcasters and broadcasters. The first is an extensive descriptive version, which goes masses similarly to OBS. The Xsplit Gamecaster is a liter model that makes specifically broadcast novices pass live quicker. The advantage is simple to manipulate, but the downside is that you can't trade the dynamics or make your broadcast your own. It is usually endorsed that you keep broadcast software program software and make investments some time. On the only hand, you may deliver masses on your web page visitors and however, you have got the possibility to make your broadcast your very very own and sync or trade it frequently.

Lightstream

Lightstream is a totally precise streaming answer as it uses cloud-based totally completely completely generation to deal with a massive amount of your flow into encoding, which reduces the strain to your hardware. In stay streaming programs, it is new browser-based totally combat.

Lightstream lets in you to begin streaming freely and now not the usage of a down load, no technical facts required, and outstanding of all, it's really unfastened. Lightstream includes centered settings and is included with out of doors streaming system like Streamlabs for alerts. Although it meets some of the easy requirements for gaming streams, the Lightstream can moderate up the audio gadget or podcasts.

One super characteristic is being capable of fast deliver the link to the traveller, and Lightstream will glide their video and audio feed right away in your waft with none confusion spherical. However, there may be a drawback that in the unfastened version there are a few regulations on functions. Free Lightstream customers are confined to 30 FPS and 720P identical because the XSplit Broadcaster. Also, you can skip excellent for 3 hours besides which you motion with Lightstream integration on Mixer. To enhance the fee is rather excessive, it comes in at $ 89 a month if you pay for a 12 months.

Chapter 7: Hardware You Need To Have For Streaming On Twitch

Choosing your hardware is each other vital step. To begin with Streaming, you need to first bring together the specified hardware or, if it already exists, take a look at if it's miles sufficient to fulfill your features or not. First, it's far vital to recognize wherein medium you want to circulate in. It creates a distinction both you need to circulate the game out of your computing device, console, or cellular telephone. There are numerous settings on the manner to edit your setup for streaming on Twitter. The incredible abilities to don't forget while getting your hands at the hardware are:

•Excellent streaming cameras

•Advanced streaming microphone

•Excellent streaming headsets

Whilst the console of video video video games like Play Station or Xbox is prepared with the entirety had to make certain easy Streaming, it is not the identical at the PC, due to the fact there are an entire lot of hardware components in every PC.

PC streaming necessities:

When it involves hardware as with each video video video video games you purchase have certain necessities, Streaming is also the same. There is a bit rundown given on the most vital things to search for and what simple desires you have to meet.

CPU: When locating a CPU, you need to endure in thoughts going for an AMD Ryzen 5 and an Intel i5. A minimal need to be the quad-middle. 6 and above cores are suitable, as your CPU is chargeable for gameplay and coding every. If the CPU is not strong, your flow can be suffered from stutters.

GPU: The essential problem on the same time as considering the GPU is figuring out the video video video games you like to play on the machine. Also, the RAM should be 4GB at the least or greater. If your CPU isn't always the maximum effective, you need to endure in mind investing in a sturdy GPU, because the GPU moreover appears after the manner of encoding, and because of this the strain at the CPU is decreased. A inclined GPU can purpose frame bargain, failure, and inside the worst-case scenario actually actually fails. Models which might be endorsed the most encompass Nvidia GTX 1650 Super (AMD-Pendant: Radeon RX 5600) or RTX 2600 Super (AMD-Pendant: RX 5700), each rocking with 8GB.

Memory (RAM): Almost all techniques in your gadget are bogged down thru the dearth of memory. At least 8GB of reminiscence, on the identical time as 16+

is usually advocated as your RAM has severa artwork to do in any case. You additionally should purchase a pre-built PC in case you do not understand which one to get in terms of building pc structures.

A strong dependable net connection

Your net speed topics the mot in Streaming. Having first-rate hard wares with a awful internet does not make a top notch combo. All of your effective hardware may be insignificant if your net is walking low. In the surrender not nice the pc's average normal performance topics but additionally the net connection. The first high-quality concept given via manner of the experts isn't always to use a wi-fi net connection, but a cable connection. In this manner, the relationship can be strong and there might be no body loss or packet loss.

The body rate implies what number of photos are being made at a given time and, as a broadcaster is being broadcast. That's why you need to make sure a excessive fantastic of the frame, to ensure your broadcast does now not lag and is good to look at. Ideally, you check 60 frames in step with second (fps).

Also, pictures want to be of excessive decision as it is able to float as plenty as 720p desire as much as the extent of accomplice/associate, a well-known Internet connection should be a way inside the beginning. Once you have got performed this, you need to circulate at 60fps with 1080p selection. To achieve all of this alongside side playing a web recreation, your add pace is vital. Your stream ought to be uploaded with none interruption, which isn't feasible with a sixteen Mbit connection. A minimal of fifty Mbit connection is wanted.

A microphone and headset

All professional settings are organized with a microphone and headset. The entire Streaming is based totally on Seeing and paying attention to and they are the actual hobby-changers in Streaming. You should make certain that those should be of the great tremendous. But it does now not imply you need to positioned plenty of stress on your pocket. You can definitely get a package deal deal at surely cheap fees.

Streaming is beyond playing a online game. Excellent broadcasting is likewise involved - they inject amusing, funny, and subtle feedback into their streams and engage lots with their site visitors. Sound is the maximum crucial device you use to speak collectively with your goal marketplace, and not anything is stressful than looking a clean go along with the float with out a audio and no man or woman is interested in searching such bored streams. Everyone desires a few noise and humor. A first rate way to talk with visitors is with the aid of way of voice (in comparison to typing - use your keyboard handiest to play a recreation), so that you need to have a high-quality microphone for that. You ought to furthermore buy a decent exceptional headset that lets you pay interest your pastime sounds with out sending any remarks to the microphone. Using a integrated microphone on your laptop or webcam isn't in any respect recommended due to the fact it may even select the sound of keyboard clicks because it's close to the keyboard and a long way from the mouth.

Webcam

It is a well-known opinion that webcam is the most critical trouble to have even as doing Streaming, but they will be incorrect. Most laptops include their blanketed webcams nowadays, and at the same time as this could be sufficient when you have a set charge variety, however in near future, you ought to look to put money into a exceptional net virtual virtual camera on the way to allow you to reveal off your lovely face to all viewers. The webcam is optionally available, but people are curious to appearance your expressions and what you appear to be even as streaming and the way you react to humans's remarks on display. The broadcast receives very famous if you show your face. Remember to keep exquisite in your thoughts whilst attempting to find an appropriate webcam. Look for webcams with covered encoders. Some webcams have this feature. If your webcam does now not have it, streaming pressure falls at the laptop. Well, that is great, but it takes a number of the computer's sources.

Some accessories

If your gaming software program, hardware, digicam, microphone, and are all got to work, you have to additionally cope with various things that can provide you with a profits and make you appearance extra expert for your twitch declares. Some terrific picks to bear in mind are;

Mouse, Mousepads - They each are rather recommended.

Headphones - If you do not use a headset, having terrific headphones (or earphones) will do wonders now not excellent in your broadcast but also to your recreation.

Extension cables and USB cables - all of at the manner to make your table cleanser and the cables/cables wires will no longer be capable of gain wherein they need to transport, Amazon can likely be your splendid pal for buying this.

Second Monitor - It can be used to display your streaming fitness, manage your music, and feature a study all chat messages and is extraordinarily endorsed, or in case you can't discover the cash for you could go cheaper and use the Twitch app through manner of downloading it in your cell phone.

Lights

Each room has a fantastic look where the gaming is set up. Daylight comes indifferently, one character prefers it to be dark, a few other vibrant, or the opportunity depending on day and night time. To avoid this, mild boxed must be used. This illuminates the motion region and we need to your target marketplace watch you inside the mild. For a truthful mild distribution, use as a minimum bins: one within the returned of your desk and the other on the left. This lets in in identifying the time of day, alternatives for darkish or moderate rooms, and the constellation of domestic home windows. In this way, you offer the same photograph to every broadcast on Facecam. This is the most appropriate generation.

Green show screen

The magic trick is the inexperienced screen that every professional broadcaster uses. If you do no longer like your room's records or don't want the net square box, use the famous green statistics. Founded in Hollywood, it's far regardless of the reality that a staple of current-day digital broadcasting. And no longer like exceptional streaming media on Twitch, the green display display is one of the most inexpensive purchases, however at a miles better rate because it the simplest with a view to deliver you extra site visitors and fans.

Stream Deck

Streamer's pleasant pal is the glide deck. There are unique forms of decks for anyone to be had. The streaming computing tool is the identical of your deck placed and subsequent to the video display devices and another streaming setup. It is prepared with buttons that make streaming movements tons much less complex, it makes life on Twitch a whole lot less difficult. For example, overlays can be changed you could blur outside and inside, or you could write something on your ongoing go together with the float like you may factor out hyperlinks of your social media profiles. Each button can be customized and is visually and functionally attractive. The buttons are with smaller digital indicates so the latter is viable. This manner, the hooked up software can be used to customise the icon that fits you high-quality. The telephone also may be used as a circulate. However, it's miles advocated you get a flow into deck quick to keep away from any hustle. Choosing the proper hardware for Streaming also can appear daunting, so there can be a compiled listing of encouraged constructing materials to help you get started.

Chapter 8: Purpose

Have Purpose

•To enhance the opportunities of fulfillment at a task, we ought to first apprehend the purpose why we are doing this venture. What is the purpose?

•Why does this take into account? Why no longer just pass this economic catastrophe and circulate proper away to the summary of all of the strategies in Chapter sixteen? The cause topics for severa motives

1.Motivation - we need to apprehend why we are preventing for a few issue. We must direct our efforts at some detail: a motive. It can be a few thing, however a reason have to exist, otherwise we're out of place.

2.Focus - if we recognise what we are doing and why, then with the useful resource of proxy, we recognize what we are not doing. To succeed at a few detail calls for interest, which means saying no to topics that aren't essential. If we apprehend "the why" and apprehend what's crucial - we can attention with the useful aid of deprioritizing everything else.

3.Authenticity - searching deep down inside yourself to apprehend why you're embarking on this adventure will assist you to maintain your splendid self in advance as a creator. Authenticity is essential. Only you apprehend your proper self, and you may have a higher chance of succeeding with the useful resource of being yourself in region of appearing as someone else.

•For now, please pause and take a minute to mirror on "the why." Keep asking why till you get to what you located is the foundation cause.

•Hopefully, we are starting to set up "the why." This way also can take time, and this is okay. Once we've got got a semblance of "the why," permit's take into account our desires as a writer.

•What must achievement look like 30 days from now? What approximately 90 days? What about a yr from now?

•Why is that this crucial? First, it's critical to break down the trouble into components. The concept of becoming partnered if you are unpartnered seems big. How can I likely get there? Or the concept of streaming if you are beginning from scratch, appears equally as intimidating. That is

due to the reality each give up-states are huge dreams that include severa complicated options. Breaking them down will simplify the course ahead. It will add structure. Second, it'll permit us to have amusing some achievement early.

Celebrating wins along the way is critical for our mental fitness and strength stages.

What Are Your Strengths?

After masses of introspective digging on "the why" and tough, but essential intention placing, we've got emerge as to the amusing element. What's the plan? Who are you? Who do you need to be? Yes, extra questions, however that is essential. Authenticity is how you win. Nobody can be a better version of yourself than you, and there are a few humans obtainable that love what you need to supply ahead. Yes, you!

Before we dig into the sorts of streamers - please pause and consider what makes you enthusiastic about growing content and high-quality others? What makes you glad? What are you appropriate at?

Here are a number of the streamer instructions that exist these days. Please observe that there are numerous different lessons, and mainly, recognize that you can create your personal and be aware if people like it. When we spoke approximately motion and experiments - that's what we're speakme about. Don't be afraid to try to to fail because, on the minimal, you may look at. If you don't see a category that appeals to you, that is k. Pave your direction. These are truely alternatives.

Variety streamer

• You are activity agnostic. You dabble within the entirety or at least in pretty more than a few video video games. When a cutting-edge sport comes out, you are there gaming on day one, specifically if the community is happy.

• To succeed as a preference streamer, it'd help in case you had a person or entertainment attraction that transcends the sport. People come to take a look at your address the sport instead of the sport itself.

Specialist

• You play a selected exercise. That is your trouble. You don't necessarily want to be a top-ranked participant at this sport, however this undertaking is your information. That is what you do. You experience it. You are constructing a network spherical it.

• It might assist you be triumphant if you have been top-ranked at this recreation, but that is not a demand. You can also provide pretty a few enjoyment rate, thoughtful assessment, or network interplay.

• It is well well worth noting that for some one-trick pony streamers, that particular pastime is what got them started out, however transitioning out of that recreation might be tough. It is not unusual for one-trick pony streamers to lose web page site visitors on the same time as she/he engages in distinctive content.

Pro

• You understand what this is. You are Pro at this recreation. Top-ranked. You don't need to be signed, however you may be true. People just like the endgame. People need to appearance a show of abilties. If you're top at a selected undertaking, you could get a popularity for that game and amplify a network together along with your sheer skills.

IRL

• You don't mind showing off your existence or debating collectively together with your community on topics. You are the display. IRL is a large and developing phase in which dad and mom are net internet web hosting talk indicates, dancing, commenting on humorous films, and so much extra.

• To attain IRL, you need to no longer be shy in the front of the virtual digital camera!

Arts and Crafts

• You have a functionality or interest out of doors of gaming, and you want to percent this with the region. This capabilities can be coding, painting, cooking, making an investment, composing tune, gambling chess or poker, singing. You may be in your laptop or not. The primary variable is that this isn't always a video game.

• To be successful, you have to have a interest/activity which you are obsessed with and need to percentage. Competition on this area goes to be smaller than streaming video games, and you is probably surprised with the resource of the growth. If you've got a hobby, encourage you to take the plunge, run an test in which you circulate that for 4 weeks, and be aware what takes vicinity.

Talk display host

• You run a display or a podcast. You are opinionated, articulate, and you can get visitors on the display to talk approximately particular topics. Talk indicates are another speedy-developing section.

• To be successful, you need to have a passion for debate, a aspect of view on what it method to create a captivating communicate show, and ideally some connections to get an initial set of visitors on the display

• Note that, inside the beginning, this might be tough, specially when you have a small community. Beggars can't be choosers, and also you need to begin someplace. That is adequate. Everyone starts someplace. You will face damaging choice in web site site visitors meaning the traffic you want aren't available, and dad and mom you don't want as loads will say sure. That is also k. Keep pushing, reflect onconsideration on exciting subjects, without a doubt do your homework in advance than each show to be informed on the guest(s) and the topic of the display.

These are really some of the diverse archetypes. There are many others. The beauty of this is that there can be someone reachable who will love what you create. What is it going to be?

Goal Setting

To ruin down the problem into additives, we want dreams for every component. To have fun your small wins - we want goals.

Goal placing movements us in advance and continues us accountable. It prevents us from aimlessly flailing. It continues our ego in check.

So, as we got all the way down to develop from X to 10M fans or a few issue your cease-cause is, permit's speak about motive putting.

Set clean dreams. There ought to be as little ambiguity as viable at the same time as you get to the aim. Did you be successful or fail? Both are ok. For instance, the cause of turning into the maximum famous author is vague. How will we define the maximum well-known? Which platform? In what genre? The intention of turning into the maximum famous IRL creator is also ambiguous. We although do not recognize what recognition way, and we do no longer apprehend the time horizon. Here are examples of unique, clean desires:

- Get to 100 lovers in next 30Days

- Miss <5% of streaming commands that I decide to in my time table over the subsequent 30Days

- Maintain >0 concurrency for ten consecutive days

- Do at the least one collaboration with every other author this vicinity.

The desires must be pretty capability but bold. Do now not set unrealistic desires, but constantly try and push yourself. Become the primary writer on YouTube might be a bit an excessive amount of of a stretch for maximum humans. At the identical time, don't be afraid to fail and try and benefit topics which is probably outdoor your consolation place. If you're already averaging 10 concurrent visitors, your next cause shouldn't be 12 - allow's pass for 50. Goals are deeply non-public, and it's far difficult to offer particular recommendation. The one issue that we're in a role to mention is if dubious, shoot higher. Be bold!

Break them down into additives. Long-time period and short-term. That's right. We noted this loads. We had the planner workout. It is crucial, so we're capable of hold bringing it up. Why? Because the direction you are on goes to be tough. Growing as a author is difficult. Doing something worthwhile is tough. And so, you absolutely want to damage down your route into components to keep away from getting lost, to prevent dropping morale, and to maintain your self responsible. The identical way that video games have checkpoints. Let's pick out out a bigger purpose which you have and purpose to interrupt it down into at least 3 elements. What does that appear like?

Actionable. A well-known stoic philosopher believed that the main venture in life is to understand what we are able to and can not manipulate and then determine moves. This awareness is undying, and it applies right here because we should now not choose out desires on which we can not act. We have to be able to act. Do a few detail that is within our control. Make progress toward that intention. If you do not see a easy list of moves that you could take to get to that aim - you need to rethink your motion plan or pick out out out a taken into consideration one among a type purpose. Bottom line: avoid choosing dreams that aren't actionable.

Do no longer conflate dreams with desires. Goals are matters that you in reality want. Desires are exquisite to have. All human beings have many goals. Take a couple of minutes to reconcile your goals and desires. Desire does now not always endorse that it is materialistic. A cause can also be materialistic. You ought to have an surrender reason of making $a million as a writer, and this is your prerogative. The crucial undertaking proper here is to prioritize. It is as much as you to decide out what you need and what's superfluous. You can't have the entirety.

Write down your goals. This is a clean however vital concept.

Why write them down? First, writing provides clarity. It forces you to crystallize your mind. When putting desires - clarity is crucial. Second, it continues you honest.

Execute. Don't be a dreamer. That's proper - do the artwork. Act.

Fail. And in case you fail, that is k, but at the least you tried. Everyone desires to be the following celeb creator, but few want to place within the artwork. What are you doing in recent times to get that 1% growth in lovers? What are you doing this week? What actions are you taking? Yes, it is tough. Yes, you may fail, but without execution and motion, your desires are sincerely desires. Writing down clean, unique, and actionable dreams is a need to. Take the time to do that. That locations you earlier of many. Now, make sure that they do not turn out to be desires on a quite whiteboard that you purchased or a listing on an Instagram positioned up. Turn your dreams into effects or lessons (disasters). Now - you have to do the artwork to make development in competition to the ones goals. Go!

Reflect and examine. Pain + Reflection = Progress. You will fail, and every failure offers a lesson and an possibility to expand. You may moreover moreover strive a new undertaking, and it acquired't paintings, and you will lose traffic. That is okay. What did you analyze? You may decide to transport to a few meetups to expand your network. It turns out that some of those were now not useful for a few detail motive. Good! So that didn't artwork, and we can now dispose of this direction from our arsenal of gear to increase, and we are able to regulate. Do we go to particular meetups to decorate our "meet-up ROI"? Do we no longer visit meet-usaat all due to the truth they impact it slow desk too much? What is the getting to know from this? Try to extract gaining knowledge of from the whole lot you do, no matter the results. It ought to be your planned exercise. And this workout, this hunt for insights, it is going that will help you expand.

Growth

Let's cowl some more techniques for increase.

Chapter 9: Analytics

Numbers do not lie. And we've set up that we need to are looking for for reality to move in advance, in any other case we wander off in our ego. So, it's far critical to check statistics to efficaciously decide how you are doing. The trouble is that to get statistics, you want traction, and there may be some individuals who are truly beginning, studying this, and thinking to themselves, "I circulate to 0 visitors every day for days. What records?" That is real. Keep at it. Keep attempting matters. Some of the records right here may not practice to you, for now. Let's undergo in mind some topics together:

• First, why are we able to want to have a take a look at statistics? Because information is an accurate instance of your development.

• Second, wherein are we able to look? There are a few places. Check out the give up of motion opinions. Check out the analytics dashboard on streamlabs.Com. Toggle to advanced view to have a look at greater advanced stats. Next, check public tracking websites together with twinge.Television or twitchtracker.Com. Why appearance there? You can see how others are doing. You can benchmark yourself. You can research.

• Next, as with every data - you need to have a question you need to answer. Here are the principle questions we might be asking ourselves if we had been looking at our analytics dashboards:

o Am I progressing? The range that I care maximum approximately: fans, concurrent visitors, and so on. - how is it changing over the years? o When I see modifications in that quantity through the years - can I attribute it to anything that I did? If so - repeat it. If now not - keep attempting and analyzing. O What video games or what sports activities sports are having the maximum enormous effect on my goals and my dispositions?

• In sum, keep on foot experiments, searching at information to validate your theories, and keep attempting.

Expanding outside your present day-day platform

Twitch is in advance of any other platform in recent times with the aid of way of the usage of the number one metric that topics the most to any streamer - site visitors. However, extraordinary systems are gaining momentum. They are improving monetization, writer help, tech. They have emerge as specific content material cloth to pressure traffic. We aren't going to speak approximately the professionals and cons of every platform. There are many special critiques on this, and this is past the scope of this e-book.

While we've got have been given your interest, we need to make best one thing this is steady with the relaxation of the fabric proper right here.

• Experiment! Let's say you commenced out on Mixer. Why no longer strive Twitch? Or what in case you and all your buddies are on Twitch? Why now not attempt Facebook or YouTube? There is a rate to each experiment (a while and electricity), but we think it's well well worth including for your boom plan and seeing what takes region. Some services let you transport to a couple of platform. It is well well worth attempting them out and seeing in that you resonate most.

Collaborations

We regularly rely on the assist of various human beings whilst taking over non-trivial tasks. Collaborations inner the author environment are commonplace exercise.

Let's in short harm it down.

• Why? Feed off every different and extend. Reach new audiences. Learn a few factor new. Meet new human beings. Connect with others. Just assist. Why now not?

• How? Join corporations. Try Reddit, Discord, or be a part of groups like TwitchKittens or the Facebook Creator organization. If you google - you could discover them. Be selective in what you be a part of, but do recall it. Another way is to reap out right away and construct a relationship. You can do that via Twitter or Discord. You can also go to meetings and meet humans there. There is a higher fee right right here, however there are few substitutes for meeting humans head to head. Ultimately, the element is to area your self to be had.

• What to count on? You can count on rejection. You can assume to provide without getting a whole lot lower once more. Both are ok. It's a part of the gadget. Do no longer appearance beforehand to every body to welcome you with hands large open. Everyone is amazing. There is constrained obligation on line, and so not the entirety may be smooth, however in case you technique everything with a pleasing mind-set and supply to the human beings - desirable things will come.

• What precisely will we do as soon as we be part of? Many subjects! Ask every different for advice. Ask for techniques. Act as assist for each other. Play together or circulate together. Raid and host every other. Do Instagram takeovers or social media collaborations. Ultimately, you could aid every one-of-a-kind, and possibly even create something new.

• What is the most vital detail to hold in mind? What is the #1 problem at the same time as you try to assemble a network? The #1 element is to offer. Give to accumulate. Host others. Give proper recommendation and assist others. The vicinity is massive. Helping others expand is part of existence. The author area isn't zero-sum, due to this your benefit isn't always a person else's loss. Remember that, and if you have energy and could strength, try assisting any other writer.

• So, in brief, located your self to be had and proactively supply to others, and top topics will seem!

Discord

• Make your discord server. It doesn't keep in mind how small you're. Someone cares approximately you and your content material cloth, and that they need a place to engage with you and to interact with others who enjoy your content material fabric.

• There are many guides on a manner to installation a discord server, so we're capable of not undergo this here. Our crucial advice right proper right here is to consider moderation and your emblem. Your network is an extension of your brand. It might also additionally seem ambitious to think about your logo when you have few enthusiasts, however prolonged-term wondering pays off! Start considering your community and the manner you need to reveal up in recent times so you can grow the next day.

Chapter 10: Events And Conferences

• Attending conferences is a lot of amusing and could can help you growth, research, and increase your community. A convention can deliver new enterprise possibilities, contacts, collaborations, and the whole lot else in among. We talked about collaborations and networking, and the concern there's to place yourself to be had. Attending conferences is a positive way to region your self available. There are severa conferences that creators attend. Some well-known meetings embody PAX, TwitchCon, Blizzcon.

• When searching for to determine out whether or not or not to wait a convention, you need to be very planned collectively together with your goals. Notice a subject? Try to take a few minutes and write down precisely what you need to attain. Why waft?

Be honest with your self. Is it to have amusing? That's wonderful. Life is brief. We want to experience it. Connecting with different creators or speakme to creators you recognize or getting nearer with video games you love - that's top notch! Is it to speak with others? Okay positive. With who? Are they going? Will they be there to make sure the adventure isn't always in useless? How do you de-danger that? Getting sponsored? Good cause. Who do you need as your sponsor? Can you do pre-work earlier than the conference to constant a meeting? Once you determine out the dreams, you can determine for your self whether or now not the journey is well really worth it

• Please preserve in mind a few matters on fee. First, there is an opportunity fee, particularly for meetings. When you're there - you are likely no longer streaming or reading. Second, it's going to typically be extra pricey than you envision. If you're quick on coins - this can not be the extremely good investment. Third, if the motive is to community, those gadgets usually take severa pre-artwork and publish-art work. We aren't discouraging you from going, but we do need to set the proper expectancies that you aren't likely to attend TwitchCon and come out with a Red Bull sponsorship.

Social media

• Social media may be simple. Set it up. Get it achieved! If you haven't completed this however, make this an motion item this week. Do this before you do discord. Make this part of your boom plan.

• First - why the urgency? Because you want to start talking with the place approximately your glide. The #1 character that should be selling your self is you, and the very best way to try this is through

Twitter or Instagram. Next, you need to say your handles. People are making money owed every day. The longer you wait - the masses less probably the account you need can be to be had.

• Next - which networks? In order of precedence: Twitter, Instagram, Facebook. If you need to do TikTok or different structures - bypass for it, however as with everything, it takes time. If you do one issue - do Twitter because of the truth this is most well-known in the author and gaming community for announcements and due to the truth the content fabric is written (Instagram and TikTok will take extra paintings).

• Lastly, what do you publish? A safe preference is to provide human beings heads up while you skip live. When you try this - you need to attempt to encompass more statistics than <Hey, I am stay>. Something like <Hey/I am streaming XYZ

from A to B time, hoping to hit X# enthusiasts at some stage in the motion. Come keep out!>. Of direction - placed up a few issue authentically represents you. Jokes, memes, property you discover exciting, circulate highlights.

Hardware

Let's cover the system. Whether you pastime, do talk suggests, or IRL - you will need hardware. The purpose why this is vital is that sure topics are barebones. They are your lifeline. You can't create with out those gadget. Examples are a laptop, a cellular phone, or Streamlabs OBS. And positive subjects will come up with an issue, specifically in case you are a gamer. An example is a splendid mouse and mousepad. An element for your pastime will have a effective dating for your boom, and given that this ebook is set boom - we're able to cowl hardware in short.

One compulsory disclaimer in advance than we dig in. Everyone's goals, opportunities, and situations are special. We may additionally disagree on what's the extremely good GPU or mouse or mic, and that is k. Take the entirety we're saying with a grain of salt, shape your very personal beliefs, and act. The one thing that isn't up for debate is that during a vacuum, extra money gets you better equipment near hardware. Everyone's financial situation is particular. That is life. If you are not capable of discover the money for some of the subjects we speak right right right here - that is flawlessly ok. You can do first-rate matters with what you have got.

Note: in case you are a content author who isn't always a gamer, numerous this segment will now not be applicable. You are welcome to bypass. We are such as this section truely due to the fact many folks that are aiming to be live-streaming content material material creators come from the gaming records.

Keyboard:

•A mechanical keyboard is advanced to the non-mechanical keyboard. The motive is -fold. First, your input registers better. There is plenty less chance of a misclick. Second, it is lots greater durable. Your AWSD will no longer put on out.

•We suggest a stressed out keyboard due to the reality it is one a super deal much less element to endure in mind. Batteries may moreover die. There might be greater latency. A keyboard is one of the areas wherein you want to be stable than sorry.

•There are volumes written about the mechanical keyboards and the switches, so moving into-intensity proper right here is beyond the scope of this e-book. We recommend you try a few out and notice what tactile remarks you pick out.

Mouse:

•Similar tale as with a keyboard. We recommend you get a mouse designed for gamers. Why? It can be extra dependable. It will revel in higher. It will be more durable. The teams that growth gaming mice interview and have a look at dozens of professional game enthusiasts to align on the format, look, remarks, buttons for those mice. These mice are designed with a gamer in thoughts.

•Our non-public choice is to choose out a burdened out mouse. The primary reason is the price.

•Adjusting your mouse settings, specially DPI, is a few element you may and need to do while you buy the mouse. This is a purpose to put money into a gaming mouse in place of the mouse that ships together together with your PC. Typical gaming mice in recent times come with software program software custom-designed to tweak the settings.

Mousepad:

•Mousepads are a critical component that many neglect approximately, specially if you are attempting to excel at a selected pastime genre. Gaming mousepads are not costly however will circulate a protracted way to enhance your gameplay and ordinary consolation.

•Consider a particular mousepad size for specific genres. FPS players are diagnosed to have the most important surface region for their mousepad for a reason. They want a entire form of motion while monitoring a player. You can pick out out a unique mousepad length based on the sport you pick out, or you can moreover pick out a giant carpet-like mouse on the way to offer you sufficient room for any game. You never must fear about sliding off.

Gaming headset:

•Another important tool. Now we're moving into components of your setup which can be beneficial for all and sundry - no longer actually game enthusiasts. If you propose on doing a whole lot of talk shows, you could want to invest in a mic which incorporates Yeti, but a headset with right audio is a extremely good start.

•You need to be audible, and you want to pay attention. You may be a part of discord corporations and scrims at the side of your network. You are speaking on your chat. There may be plenty extra on that in upcoming sections

•The backside line - a headset is important. Here are 3 key subjects to maintain in thoughts: comfort and pressured out vs. Wireless. On consolation - we propose analyzing evaluations and ideally trying out the device. If you order some aspect and it does no longer wholesome properly on your ears. Return it. It is okay. Few things are greater stressful than feeling as though your headset is heating your head or sliding. Wired vs. Wi-fi is a easy preference based totally mostly on all the studies we've achieved. We advocate wi-fi.

Monitor:

•The #1 maximum essential aspect for a gaming display is the refresh charge. Do no longer anticipate that better selection or a bigger show period always way better. A big show can refresh poorly and could make the game seem jarring. There are three number one refresh fee gradients, and every one will charge extra cash. We can't will permit you to recognise what to select, but what we are capable to mention is that the most big differentiating difficulty a number of the video display gadgets, in particular from a gamer's thoughts-set, is the refresh fee.

•Folks care approximately decision, aesthetic, brand. These topics do rely for a few, and it's miles absolutely as much as you what you choose. For instance, if you decide you need to play many tables of on-line poker on one show - resolution is probably greater relevant to you.

PC

•Configuring a gaming or a streaming PC is beyond the scope of this ebook. There are troves of recommendation on this. Budget and your desires is probably the maximum massive factors. We do want to call out three topics: GPU, CPU, and RAM

•GPU is crucial. GPUs collect massive enhancements lots much less frequently then CPU and RAM, so making an funding in a GPU today method that it'll possibly be greater relevant for an prolonged time. As a gamer, if there can be one region which you need to invest in - it is probably the GPU. As a non-gamer, a GPU can be an entire lot less relevant.

•RAM is likewise essential. A smooth way to consider RAM is multitasking. How many concurrent matters do you generally do? You have your pastime, Streamlabs OBS, browser with many tabs, discord, what else? You do no longer need to skimp on RAM.

•CPU. Similar tale because the RAM except that CPU is the one area out of the 3 that gets the most common improvements (appearance up Moore's regulation). You want enough to beneficial aid your sports, however you probably do no longer need lots of center with the present day-day Intel or AMD chips.

Chapter 11: General Set-Up

•The splendor of this segment is that, for the maximum component, that is all internal your manipulate. That's proper! General set-up of your desk can also appear like a small trouble, however it's far crucial because of the truth little matters compound to extra large items in the end.

•There are 3 key topics that we endorse.

1. Maintain a display at eye degree. You do no longer want a flowery display stand or arm for this. You can use books. Place a few books below your show to wholesome your eye stage on the same time as you are sitting down immediately (key!). Why? Avoid slouching. Good posture is not genuinely beneficial on your fitness but will placed you more inside the location. When you're sitting upright and gift - you're organized to have interaction at a hundred%, whether or not or no longer or

not it's miles a interest or a podcast or a few issue else.

2. Make first-rate there is a ways among you and the display. You need to maintain your eyesight. Plus, it's going to make it hard to technique your show display in case you are too close to.

three. Finally, if you are the use of a gaming chair or an place of job chair that has reclining capability - don't forget setting that to an upright angle. Your default position need to now not be slouching, and even as you are sitting upright and engaged - you'll be extra alert. All the small subjects upload up, allow's start the day strong!

•Bonus, if possible and fantastic, this one prices coins - don't forget making an investment in a status table! Studies show that these are right for you.

Software

So, you've made your choices on hardware. Now it's time to speak about software program application. Here we'll speak about the critical software you may want to get started out. Like hardware, all and sundry may have remarkable situations that require particular unique goals, so right here we'll talk the software as a manner to be the maximum useful to the most people.

Full Transparency - as you may recognize, at Streamlabs, we're a crew of stay streamers building software program to empower creators. We placed blood, sweat, and tears into each of our products, and that is why we are the most famous solution. The backside line is that we're going to be inherently biased even as we communicate software program program, but we moreover without a doubt trust in our tools. As usually, you want to make your personal selections.

Platform:

•The platform you pick to start stay streaming is a extraordinary and interesting selection. You possibly already have a platform in thoughts as you have a look at this.

•Some of the questions you need to be asking as you choose out out a platform:

•What are the streaming structures which might be to be had in my geography? O Do I already have a following on a platform that facilitates stay streaming? O Is there a particular platform in which the shape of content material cloth I desire to create is prospering?

•Do I certainly have friends or a network that would assist me get began out on a selected platform?

•We advise multistreaming to multiple systems as you get began out. Starting this manner permits you to reap as many capacity visitors as feasible. It's tough to expect the platform wherein you may find out an target market and make bigger your community, so developing your odds with the useful useful resource of multistreaming is an outstanding manner to start. While hard inside the beyond, this is now fairly clean with tools just like the local multistream function we offer at Streamlabs.

Broadcast Software:

•Your broadcast software program is the glue that brings collectively your pastime, webcam, out of doors video feeds, and so forth. And publicizes them in your streaming platform(s).

•Be cautious of buying broadcast software program program software – nearly all streamers are the use of loose broadcasting software, and also you need to be capable of do the identical.

•Some of the capabilities you have to consider while you pick out your broadcasting software program: o Themes and format help to assist make your flow into stand out and look professional.

•Ease of use and customer support and documentation to help you troubleshoot. O Performant and reliable, especially vital in case you plan to apply the same computer for specific responsibilities like playing a game. O Integration with the opportunity software program application utility you'll want to live movement: the systems you flow into to, tools to have interaction your viewers and monetize, system that will help you mild your go with the flow.

•Will the software program software scale with you, permitting you to growth your manufacturing quality with capabilities like an app hold.

•Our advice is our center product, Streamlabs OBS, we've attempted to assemble the most sturdy all-in-one answer for live streaming. With talents like neighborhood multistream and being totally backed up on the cloud, we've made it clean to get began inside the splendid way feasible. Many systems advocate Streamlabs OBS due to the fact the recommended broadcast software software utility.

Alerts and Donations:

•Alerts and donations are crucial in helping you increase your target market and monetize your circulation no matter the streaming platform.

•Alerts supply your traffic a hazard to be diagnosed on flow for their actions that support you. On go with the flow appreciation with indicators provides reciprocal price to you and your website visitors.

•You need to set signals for all of the movements that depend to you, platformspecific actions like follows or subs, and monetization indicators for donations and merch purchases.

•Donations are the direct line of monetization among you and your visitors. Users will frequently ask questions, percent media, and so on. With their donations. It's vital to embody a hyperlink for your donation net web page in a distinguished area for your channel, so it's clean on your goal market to discover.

•Donations and indicators are controlled thru Streamlabs. We don't acquire any expenses in your viewer's donations and assist multiple price strategies across the globe. We additionally provide specific equipment like a charity platform to mechanically modify your donations and signals to help charity streams in seconds.

Chat Bot:

•For maximum structures, a speak bot is a useful device that servesvital functions: moderation of your circulate's chat and engagement in your web site site visitors.

•Automated moderation of your flow into's chat is essential to hold your channel's content material material open to a broader target market and ensuring your chat is complying with Terms of Service on fine systems.

•Engaging your visitors in giveaways, video video video games, and answering fundamental questions all help maintain your target audience engaged and improves their revel in in your channel.

•As you increase your channel, your chat bot becomes increasingly more crucial, so we advocate getting started out with one from the start allowing you to get greater cushty with the abilities and device as you broaden.

•At Streamlabs, we offer an excellent chat bot, Streamlabs Cloudbot, this is subsidized up inside the cloud and gives a simply dependable and sturdy feature set.

Mobile Streaming:

•It's an interesting time for cellular stay streamers. As both the hardware and software program program have visible big improvement in cutting-edge years.

•It is important to have software this is reliable and meets your particular desires to stay skip effectively.

•We strongly propose the Streamlabs cellular app. It gives a few very contemporary skills like concurrently streaming each your digital camera and capturing your display on the equal time. Many streaming structures advise the Streamlabs mobile app because the desired manner to flow into. There are top magnificence capabilities available, like disconnect protection, which preserves your glide if you lose sign, this prevents losing your web page site visitors.

Optics

Why now not just release into growing greater special content material cloth? You have the vision, you apprehend what you're going for, you have the sport plan damaged down into elements. Should we in fact move-live in Streamlabs OBS? Sure - cross for it. If there may be one assignment matter that you will see in this e-book, it's far that motion creates effects. The excellent way to begin is to…. Begin.

However, if/at the same time as making a decision you have were given time - we do advise you invest in optics. Invest for your appearance. Invest in how you come back off along hundreds of various streamers who're vying for viewer interest. Invest in the first effect. First impressions are frequently last impressions.

Before we get into the diverse subjects you can do to beautify optics, permit's in quick talk about the approach. Our philosophy for boom and for every motion we take is thoughtful motion and calculated dangers. This isn't any wonderful.

• "The why" right right here is 3-fold. First, we need to make an top notch first have an effect on. Second, we need to face out amongst others. We want to be effects discoverable and notable. Third, we want to look expert. If you install effort into a few aspect - it'll pay off. Everything topics, together with appearance. Yes, your gameplay, your charisma, your power ranges - these are the primary factors, however how your motion appears will add rate.

• "The how" echoes points made in advance, but they'll be so vital that we want to hold cementing them in workout. "The how" right here is circulate! Do it. Try embracing some of the optic thoughts we communicate beneath. Just attempt. There is not any need to attempt to do it . Don't fear about spending days on a wonderful set-up with all custom panels, emojis, overlays, witty titles, and masses of others. You can start small however start. See what takes vicinity. Perhaps you narrow up the optic venture into many subtasks and see what takes vicinity?

Chapter 12: Get Expert Looking Overlays

Streamlabs OBS gives every loose and paid overlays. You can begin with unfastened, but we do advocate you which you choose an overlay this is cohesive and, at the minimal, informs the viewer of even as you're approximately to start. This is important because of the truth not handiest will your movement stand-out, however you can growth the possibility of getting some site visitors in advance than you start. Put yourself within the triumphing feature from the beginning. Everything subjects.

Customize your indicators. Yes, default indicators work, but you can

create some thing non-public. Again, it doesn't need to be a fancy image. It may be a meme or a gif of you or some thing specific for your community like an internal comic story. Don't have a community but - that's good enough. You are to your way. You need to begin somewhere! Pick a few component that appeals to you and make it your alert. Then bypass

similarly and create unique signs for considered one of a kind event kinds. Recognize your web site traffic, and they may recognize you.

Invest for your "approximately" phase. Yes, it's a few traces of text, but (1) first impressions are on occasion the final, (2) each detail subjects. Let's located ourselves inside the shoes of the viewer (proper exercising while thinking via maximum selections). After you choose to take a look at a waft that caught your hobby, wherein do you move next? Most people will skim the about section. Who are you? Why are you right here? What do you need to inform the arena? Make this section you. Just make sure that you don't write an essay.

Add relevant panels. This is maximum applicable if you are a

Twitch/Mixer streamer; on exclusive platforms, we propose you add extra links. Often large-time streamers have sponsors here. Let's expect that we don't have sponsors YET, and this is good enough. Let's add some key portions: (1) streaming time desk (a want to - more on this later), (2) donation hyperlink, (three) tips (i.E., what's your network approximately, what isn't always adequate).

Think via your glide call and tags. This is

vital. It is what people see when they scroll, at the side of what you are doing glide (your interest and overlays). This is also what is going to be tagged through the use of the internet web site and will get brought about as clients are seeking. Let's set up exercisingof the ideas that we discussed above: (1) be thoughtful and deliberate approximately this - the whole thing topics, (2) check. It's ok to strive diverse subjects and notice what works. If the internet net page to that you are streaming lets in this - make certain you upload relevant tags. Tags help human beings find out you. Let's check some circulate titles that we assume are informative or smart.

Add your social networks (extra on this within the boom

bankruptcy). Let's assume that you don't have those installation but. Good! The growth assignment for week one is to create social bills (Instagram, Twitter, TikTok, Facebook, anything else that you count on will assist). Then hyperlink them. Why? First, it lets in your network live in touch with you when you aren't streaming. Every piece makes a distinction, and this may add up. Second, if you don't have the ones social bills booked but - don't wait too lengthy and get some component locked these days earlier than it gets harder to have a social account that suits your name. You want to maximise avenues to broaden your brand, and social networks are going to be this kind of avenues. Concerned that no person will look at you? That's ordinary. Why don't we allow the network decide! One element is for high-quality. If you don't make those debts, nobody will observe you.

And in case you don't begin streaming - you can never grow to be a creator, so flow into!

Community

Your network is who you do all of this for. This is the manner you growth. This is why you grow. In many techniques, it's miles your network and no longer your playstyle as a manner to define you. They are proper proper here for you, and your fulfillment is greater regularly than now not due to their love and assist. Let's damage down some tools which might be beneficial in managing and growing a community

Paying attention to speak. This is going to be the number 1 priority in any respect levels. Paying interest to talk is hypercritical. When you're for your direction to associate, each traveler is there to guide you, and you have to deliver them power. When you begin to increase and feature extra enthusiasts, it is straightforward to get stuck up in the sport or to push aside the network, but that is how matters disintegrate. So, what does being attentive to chat mean in exercising? As we said previously - there are not any silver bullets. There isn't always any if X in chat, then Y reaction. All we're able to provide you is steering and thoughts-set. General standards. In this example, taking note of chat way literary prioritizing chat and bringing energy into your interactions with chat. Greet and function fun people. Engage in their questions and ask them questions decrease again. That's right. Talk to them about their day or the surroundings or this endeavor. You want to be in the splendid-power-giving-immoderate-empathy mind-set. Let's wreck this down similarly into hassle factors and full-size concepts.

Acknowledge all of us. Give all and sundry that comes on your

circulate some hobby to the great of your capability. Some acknowledgment is higher than doing now not whatever. People love popularity and paying attention to the sound of their call. People want interest. So, permit's offer your community what they want.

Engage your website site visitors. During our interviews, we spoke with many streamers stuck at 5-10 concurrent site visitors for months. When we watched their streams, we observed that a number of them had been gambling the game and now not attractive with their chat. When we asked why - a few said that they didn't pay interest or didn't apprehend what to say. Not the whole lot is ready us. Yes, those dad and mom got here to check you play, but they may live or come another time if we communicate approximately them. People love speakme about themselves. Let's deliver them that possibility. To take this one step similarly - this will be a part of your growth plan. What if you bought right here up with a few concept-frightening questions? If now not - a clean, how is your day going, will go a protracted way.

Start a debate. You may be a moderator or the spark, however the bulk of the engagement may be viewer to viewer. That is awesome as it lets you reputation on your venture, and it acts as an avenue for site visitors to build relationships among themselves. The latter is a notable outcome. If a success, now human beings have not begun another cause to visit your channel. Previously it modified into every your character or your hobby. Now it can be because of the reality they want to engage with that viewer over again. That is a actual network. Simple questions can be to invite your chat what they think about a cutting-edge occasion in gaming, collectively with a convention or a game launch. Not excellent what's taking location? A remarkable supply can be Reddit. Go to the subreddit for a few trouble interest you have interaction in (gaming, paintings, a particular recreation, coding, political debate) and check out the pinnacle conversations.

Everyone is one in every of a type. If a few parents want to lurk or now not engage at the identical time as you greet them - this is ideal sufficient. Let them be. Our tackle this is that your default beginning stance - your setting out approach - must be immoderate electricity, warmth, non-public contact, authentic hobby. If a person does now not reciprocate, this is k. Let's allow them to lurk. Maybe they'll be now not as open, or in all likelihood you want to assemble greater rapport with them, so permit them to lurk in peace at the same time as displaying warmth and electricity.

Chat bot. Managing chat is going to be tough, particularly as you increase.

Even if you are starting out - it is beneficial to get a communicate bot. A chat bot will have interaction your web site traffic while you went on destroy or combating a md. A chat bot can tell your traffic crucial statistics approximately you or this movement on command. Some human beings pick out to engage via a communicate bot. Some are absolutely lurkers. That is good enough. Let's provide them that choice. There is also the attitude of chat moderation. We ought to abide through platform Terms of Service (greater on that later), and so a talk bot can and have to be leveraged to preserve your chat easy. Streamlabs gives a extremely good chat bot that we fairly endorse. It includes system for chat moderation, viewer engagement, polls, timers, minigames. As with all Streamlabs gear - everything is subsidized as an awful lot because the cloud, so it is available for you 24/7.

Give the regulars extra love. This is a clean issue, but it's so crucial that it deserves a selected segment. The regulars are the backbone of your community. Give them love and hobby. Ask them about their day. Greet them. If you neglected them turning into a member of chat - please take time to test chat and apprehend them. This does no longer simplest cause them to experience cherished and rewards them for being there for you. Doing this moreover suggests the rest of your community the kind of connection they may have in the event that they constantly aid you.

Play a few tune. That is some aspect we gleaned from our

research. Music doestopics:

1.Music brightens the environment - it affords electricity - even in case you aren't speakme, and the chat is silent, song will upload some charge

2.Music creates some exceptional interaction aspect among you and your network - people may want to recognize what track you are being attentive to.

Be sure to make certain you're broadcasting track you've got have been given the rights to broadcast on circulate. An clean and safe manner to do this is, is leveraging one of the top elegance music apps in the Streamlabs OBS App Store.

Acknowledge donations, stars, follows, likes, subscribers, and all of the exceptional deliberate moves that your visitors can also take to help you. This may

appear like common enjoy, however it's so crucial that we want to spend time on this. Why do that? The why is twofold: (1) first-rate reinforcement of these movements bring about extra of these moves from your community - that is a brilliant element for you, (2) giving 1:1 interest and popularity to the person who supported you inside the suggest time is the minimum you may do to reciprocate. This individual took planned movement to aid you, and there is handiest one aspect - we thank that man or woman. Make them experience precise. Make it seem like it is genuinely you and them in chat. Be thankful! Some parents can also moreover moreover lose song of this workout of thanking and acknowledging direct guide amidst a heated pastime or an inflow of beneficial aid. Putting our empathy hat on - allow's remember how it feels to take that direct supportive motion and get not something once more.

www.ingramcontent.com/pod-product-compliance
Lightning Source LLC
LaVergne TN
LVHW022315060326
832902LV00020B/3481